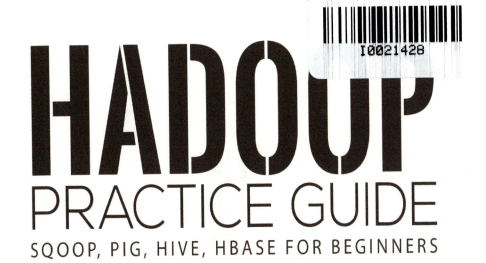

HADOOP
PRACTICE GUIDE
SQOOP, PIG, HIVE, HBASE FOR BEGINNERS

JISHA MARIAM JOSE

INDIA · SINGAPORE · MALAYSIA

Notion Press

Old No. 38, New No. 6
McNichols Road, Chetpet
Chennai - 600 031

First Published by Notion Press 2019
Copyright © Jisha Mariam Jose 2019
All Rights Reserved.

ISBN 978-1-64587-753-0

Contents

Chapter 1

Hadoop Distributions

1.1 INTRODUCTION

Hadoop is an Apache open-source framework that store and process Big Data in a distributed environment acrossthe cluster using simple programming models. Hadoop provides parallel computation on top of distributed storage.

Since Apache Hadoop is open source, many companies have developed distributions that go beyond the original open source code. This is very much similar to Linux distributions such as RedHat, Fedora, and Ubuntu. Each of the Linux distributions supports its own functionalities and features like user-friendly GUI in Ubuntu. Similarly, **Red Hat** is popular within enterprises because it offers support and also provides ideology to make changes to any part of the system at will.

Likewise, there are 3 main types of Hadoop distributions which have its own set of functionalities and features and are built under the base HDFS.

Cloudera Hadoop Distribution

Cloudera is the market trend in Hadoop space and is the first one to release commercial Hadoop distribution. It offers consulting services to bridge the gap between – "what does Apache Hadoop provides" and "what organizations need".

Cloudera Distribution is:

- **Fast for Business**: From analytics to data science and everything in between, Cloudera delivers the performance you need to unlock the potential of unlimited data.

5

- **Makes Hadoop Easy to Manage**: With Cloudera Manager, automated wizards let you quickly deploy your cluster, irrespective of the scale or deployment environment.

- **Secure without Compromise:** Meets stringent data security and compliance needs without sacrificing business agility. Cloudera provides an integrated approach to data security and governance.

Horton-Works Distribution

The Horton-Works Data Platform (HDP) is entirely an open source platform designed to manoeuvre data from many sources and formats. The platform includes various Hadoop tools such as the Hadoop Distributed File System (HDFS), MapReduce, Zookeeper, HBase, Pig, Hive, and additional components.

It also supports features like:

- HDP makes Hive *faster* through its new Stinger project.

- HDP *avoids vendor lock-in* by pledging to a forked version of Hadoop.

- HDP is focused on enhancing the *usability* of the Hadoop platform.

MapR Distribution

MapR is a platform-focused Hadoop solutions provider, just like HortonWorks and Cloudera. MapR integrates its own database system, known as MapR-DB while offering Hadoop distribution services. MapR-DB is claimed to be four to seven times faster than the stock Hadoop database, i.e. HBase, that is executed on other distributions.
It has its features like:

- It is the only Hadoop distribution that includes Pig, Hive, and Sqoop without any Java dependencies – since it relies on MapR-File System.

- MapR is the most production ready Hadoop distribution with many enhancements that make it more user-friendly, faster and dependable.

> **NOTE!!!** I have installed Cloudera platform and the hands-on practices that are shown in further chapters are with respect to Cloudera.

1.2 CLOUDERA INSTALLATION AND PRE-REQUISITES

- These 64-bit VMs require a 64-bit host OS and a virtualization product that can support a 64-bit guest OS.

- To use a VMware VM, you must use a player compatible with WorkStation 8.x or higher:

  ○ Player 4.x or higher

  ○ Fusion 4.x or higher

  Older versions of WorkStation can be used to create a new VM using the same virtual disk (VMDK file), but some features in VMware Tools are not available.

- The amount of RAM required varies by the run-time option you choose:

CDH and Cloudera Manager Version	RAM Required by VM
CDH 5 (default)	4+ GB
Cloudera Express	8+ GB
Cloudera Enterprise (trial)	10+ GB

*Minimum recommended memory. If you are running workloads larger than the examples provided, consider allocating additional memory.

Downloading a Cloudera QuickStart VM

Cloudera QuickStart VMs are available as Zip archives in VMware, KVM, and VirtualBox formats. Cloudera recommends that you use 7-Zip to extract these files, when possible. (7-Zip performs well with large files.) To download the latest VM in the required format, see Cloudera QuickStart VM Download.

QuickStart VM Software Versions and Documentation

VM Version	Documentation
CDH 5 and Cloudera Manager 5	To learn more about CDH 5 and Cloudera Manager 5, see the <u>Cloudera 5 documentation.</u> • For the latest important information about new features, incompatible changes, and known issues, see the <u>Release Guide.</u> • Cloudera Manager is installed in the VM but is turned off by default. If you would like to use Cloudera Manager, open the **Launch Cloudera Manager** icon on the desktop. Cloudera strongly recommends that before you do so, you configure the VM with a minimum of 8 GB of RAM and 2 virtual CPU cores (by default it will use 4 GB of RAM and 1 virtual CPU core). Cloudera Manager and all of the CDH services might not launch properly with less RAM. After launching Cloudera Manager, all of the services in CDH are started, although it might take several minutes for Cloudera Manager to start all of the services. To conserve resources and improve performance, Cloudera recommends that you stop services you do not plan to use. Changes made to configuration files before launching Cloudera Manager are not preserved. You can start or reconfigure any installed services using the web interface that is automatically displayed when the VM starts. **Warning:** If Cloudera Manager is running, do not use init scripts from the command line to start, stop, or configure CDH components. Doing so will leave the cluster in an undefined state that could result in data loss. Use only Cloudera Manager to start, stop, or configure CDH components when running Cloudera Manager.

QuickStart VM Administrative Information

In most cases, the QuickStart VM requires no administration beyond managing the installed products and services.

Accounts

Once you launch the VM, you are automatically logged in as the cloudera user. The account details are:

- username: cloudera
- password: cloudera
  - ○ The cloudera account has sudo privileges in the VM. The root account password is cloudera.
  - ○ The root MySQL password (and the password for other MySQL user accounts) is also cloudera.
  - ○ Hue and Cloudera Manager use the same credentials.

QuickStart VMware Image

To launch the VMware image, you will either need VMware Player for Windows and Linux, or VMware Fusion for Mac. Note that VMware Fusion only works on Intel architectures, so older Macs with PowerPC processors cannot run the QuickStart VM.

1.3 SUMMARY OF CLOUDERA INSTALLATION

Software Requirement:

- VMware Workstation Player
- Cloudera Quickstart VM

Hardware Requirement:

- RAM: Minimum 8GB
- HDD: 60GB
- Processor: Dual Core - - recommended i3, i4, i5, i7 processor

Installing VMware Workstation:

a. Download latest version of VMWare Workstation from Authorized VMWare website or other trusted website like filehippo.com

    b. Install VMWare Workstation

    c. After installation, open the VMWare through Desktop Icon or start Menu

Installing Cloudera Quickstart:

    a. Download Cloudera Quickstart VM

        1. Select any latest CDH 5 version link. *[I have downloaded Cloudera Quickstart CDH 5.13 for the exercises in this book]*

        2. Select the appropriate platform. *[in this case, it will VMWare]*

        3. Fill the registration form details, accept the agreement and click continue button. After this, download of Quickstart VM will begin.

    b. Extract Cloudera Quickstart VM through 7-zip or WinZip etc.

    c. Associate Cloudera Quickstart VM to VMWare Workstation

        1. Open the VMWare through Desktop Icon or start Menu

        2. click *"open a virtual machine"* option and browse the extracted Cloudera Quickstart VM folder location.

        3. Open the extracted folder, a required VMware supported file will be shown inside this folder. Select this file.

    d. Before starting the Cloudera Quickstart from play button, we need to change the default settings. (i.e. RAM-4GB & HDD-60 GB)

    e. Click on *"Edit Virtual Machine Setting"* option and then change the values based on your computer configuration.

        1. If your system has 16GB RAM then out of that 8GB RAM can be completely allocated to Cloudera Quickstart VM

        2. Else if the system has only 8GB RAM, then still you can work on Cloudera by allocating 5GB RAM. Here, complete 8GB is not allocated to Cloudera because by default Windows (latest Version) will be using 2GB RAM. And from remaining 6GB, we will use only 5GB for the Cloudera Quickstart VM.

    f. Once all setting is completed, start the Cloudera VM by click on *"power on this virtual machine"*

g. In this Cloudera Quickstart VM, by default

   1. Cent OS (Linux Flavour) 6.x version is installed

   2. JAVA 8 is installed

   3. MySQL is installed

   4. Cloudera 5.13 – apache Hadoop 2.7.x is installed

1.4 GENERAL INSTRUCTION ON CLOUDERA VM

a. **To verify whether required services are in good health or not**

   1. Go to browser (by default it is Firefox browser)

   2. Click on "Cloud Manager"

   3. Enter Username: cloudera

   4. Password: cloudera

   5. Click on "login"

   6. Check whether required services is in green color (good health); if no, click the corresponding actions button and restart

b. **To go through HDFS components and filesystem**

   1. Open the Firefox browser in Cloudera

   2. Click the bookmark **"Hadoop"** and select **"HDFS NameNode"** from the drop down list.

   3. On click of Overview, one can see the overview of Cloudera Quickstart and other details like – Configuration capacity, DFS used, Block pool Used, Live Nodes, Dead Nodes etc.

   4. On click of **"Datanodes"**, one can see disk usage of each DataNode, blocks used etc. In pseudo-distributed mode, there will be only one Datanaode.

   5. On click of **"Utilities"** and then **"Browse the file system"** option from the drop down, one can browse through the HDFS File System. The filesystem start from the directory root "/". Type "/" in given text box, you will see list of directories present inside the root directory.

Chapter 2

Hadoop Core Components

Hadoop is a framework that allows us to store and process large data sets in parallel and distributed fashion. The major two core components are:

1. **Hadoop Distributed File System (HDFS)** – used for storage

    It allows to dump any kind of data across the cluster. The daemons that take care of storage part are:

    a. Name Node (NN)

    b. Secondary NameNode (SNN)

    c. DataNode (DN)

2. **Map Reduce**

    It allows parallel processing of data stored in HDFS. The daemons that take care of processing part are:

    a. Job Tracker (JT)

    b. Task Tracker (TT)

2.1 DIFFERENT HADOOP MODES

Local Mode or Standalone Mode:

- Standalone mode is the default mode in which Hadoop run.

- Standalone mode is mainly used for debugging where you don't really on HDFS use.

- You can use input and output both as a local file system in standalone mode.

- You also don't need to do any custom configuration in the files – **mapred-site.xml, core-site.xml, hdfs-site.xml**.

- Standalone mode is usually the fastest Hadoop modes as it uses the local file system for all the input and output.

Pseudo-Distributed Mode:

- The **pseudo-distribute mode** is also known as a **single-node cluster** where both NameNode and DataNode will reside on the same machine.

- In pseudo-distributed mode, all the Hadoop daemons will be running on a single node. Such configuration is mainly used while testing, when we don't need to think about the resources and other users sharing the resource.

- In this architecture, a separate JVM is spawned for every Hadoop.

- component as they could communicate across network sockets, effectively producing a fully functioning and optimized mini-cluster on a single host.

- Replication Factor will be ONE for blocks.

- Changes in configuration files will be required for all the three files – **mapred-site**.xml, **core-site**.xml, hdfs-**site.xml**

Fully-Distributed Mode (Multi-Node Cluster):

- This is the **production mode of Hadoop** where multiple nodes will be running.

- Here data will be distributed across several nodes and processing will be done on each node.

- Master and Slave services will be running on the separate nodes in fully-distributed Hadoop Mode.

In the Hadoop development, each Hadoop Modes have its own benefits and drawbacks. Definitely fully distributed mode is the one for which Hadoop is mainly known for but again there is no point in engaging the resource while in testing or debugging phase. So standalone and pseudo-distributed Hadoop modes are also having their own significance.

2.2 ROLES OF VARIOUS DAEMONS

Name Node (NN):

- Allocates nodes to store data based on nearest location, network traffic. Maintains meta data like location of blocks stored, the size of the files, permissions, hierarchy etc.

- It receives heartbeat and block reports from all the nodes.

- It is a software that can be run on commodity hardware. The system having the NameNode acts as the master server and it does the following tasks:

  - Manages the file system namespace. It maintains two file namespace image and edit file log.

  - Regulates client's access to files.

  - It also executes file system operations such as renaming, closing, and opening files and directories.

Data Node (DN):

- For every node in a cluster, there will be a DataNode.

- These nodes manage the data storage of their system. DataNodes perform read-write operations on the file systems, as per client request.

- They also perform operations such as block creation, deletion, and replication according to the instructions of the NameNode.

- Generally, the user data is stored in the files of HDFS.

- The file in a file system will be divided into one or more segments and/or stored in individual data nodes.

- These file segments are called as blocks. In other words, the minimum amount of data that HDFS can read or write is called a Block.

- The default block size is 64MB, but it can be increased as per the need to change in HDFS configuration.

Secondary Name Node (SNN):

- If Name Node fails entire HDFS file system is lost. So, in order to overcome this, Hadoop implemented Secondary NameNode whose main function is to store a copy of FsImage file and edits log file.

- FsImage is a snapshot of the HDFS file system metadata at a certain point of time and EditLog is a transaction log which contains records for every change that occurs to file system metadata.

- Copies FsImage and Transaction Log from NameNode to a temporary directory.

- Merges FSImage and Transaction Log into a new FSImage in temporary directory. This process of combining edit logs with FsImage is called as checkpointing.

- Uploads new FSImage to the NameNode

  ○ Transaction Log on NameNode is purged

- Secondary NameNode takes over the responsibility of checkpointing and thus makes NameNode more available.

- It allows faster failover as it prevents edit logs from getting huge.

- Checkpointing happens periodically.

Roles of JobTracker and TaskTracker:

- A job is divided into multiple tasks which are then run onto multiple data nodes in a cluster.

- For every job submitted for execution in the system,

  ○ there is one **Jobtracker** that resides on **NameNode**

  ○ and there are **multiple Tasktrackers** which reside on **DataNode**

- It is the responsibility of Jobtracker to coordinate the activity by scheduling tasks to run on different data nodes.

- Execution of individual task is then look after by Tasktracker, which resides on every data node executing part of the job.

- Tasktracker's responsibility is to send the progress report to the Jobtracker.

- In addition, Tasktracker periodically sends **'heartbeat'** signal to the Jobtracker so as to notify him of current state of the system.

- Thus, Jobtracker keeps track of overall progress of each job. In the event of task failure, the Jobtracker can reschedule it on a different Tasktracker.

Chapter 3

Getting Started with HDFS

HDFS is the primary filesystem that Hadoop uses for MapReduce jobs. Using it is similar to using the Unix file system, so let's practice using some basic commands to become comfortable using its command line interface.

Step 1: Before executing any Hadoop commands, verify whether all the daemons are working or not by entering the following command. If no, then check the HDFS status through Cloudera Manager and restart it if required.

```
$ sudo jps
```

Step 2: The command to make NameNode leave from safemode is as follows. NameNode during its safemode collects all metadata information from the secondary NameNode.

```
$ sudo -u hdfs hdfs dfsadmin -safemode leave
```

3.1 COMMON HDFS COMMANDS

> **Note!!!**
>
> 1. All the commands can begin with "hadoop fs ...." or "hdfs dfs ...."
>
> I.e. $ Hadoop fs -ls /user/cloudera *(or)*
>
> $ hdfs dfs -ls /user/cloudera
>
> 2. In cloudera distribution, Local filesystem's default location starts from **"/home/cloudera"** and HDFS default location is **"/user/cloudera"**.

1. **Creating Your Home Directory**. To create your own home directory within the HDFS file system, enter:

```
$ hadoop fs -mkdir /user/cloudera/Practice
```

> **Note!!!** By default, permission will be denied to create a new directory in "/" and "/user" directory path. Either change the permission for these directories or use "/user/cloudera" directory path where permissions are already given

2. **Listing Your Home Directory**. To view the contents of your HDFS home directory, enter:

```
$ hadoop fs -ls /user/cloudera
```

```
drwxr-xr-x - cloudera cloudera  0 2019-05-09 02:02
    /user/cloudera/Practice
```

3. **Cat:** Copies source paths to stdout. I,e to display the file content on to the screen.

```
$ hadoop fs -cat /user/cloudera/test
```

4. **Copy a File from the Local File System into HDFS**. Before we learn how to copy a file, let's create a file named "test" to copy. Enter:

Option 1: `$ gedit test`

> An editor will be opened. Type your content, save it and then close. Control will come back to "$" prompt in terminal

Option 2: `$ echo "this is nice`

```
> nice day
> have a good day
> good morning
> file is kept in folder
> file is small" >> test
```

/* **To verify whether or not the file is created. And then read the contents through "cat" command***/

```
$ ls
$ cat test
```

```
this is nice
nice day
have a good day
good morning
file is kept in folder
file is small
```

Option 3: $ cat>test

```
this is good
good day
have a nice day
good morning
file is kept in folder
file is small
^C
```

/* To verify whether or not the file is created. And then read the content through "cat" command*/

```
$ ls
$ cat test
```

```
this is good
good day
have a nice day
good morning
file is kept in folder
file is small
```

Copy Commands for Copying File from Local File System to HDFS

```
$ hadoop fs -copyFromLocal test
(or)
$ hadoop fs -copyFromLocal test /user/cloudera
(or)
$ hadoop fs -copyFromLocal /home/cloudera/test
/user/cloudera
```

```
$ <Hadoop> <filesystem> -<command to copy>
  <source path of file to be copied> <destination
  location in HDFS>
```

- If you are already in source location then mention only filename as source path else you need to mention the complete actual path.
- By default, the destination location in HDFS is set as /user/cloudera. So, it is optional to mention this path. Whereas you need to mention the complete path if destination path is different from the default one.

To Verify Whether the Local File Is Loaded into Hadoop File System

```
$ hadoop fs -ls /user/cloudera
```

```
-rw-r--r-- 1 cloudera cloudera 121 2019-05-09 16:32
  /user/cloudera/test
```

To Check the Content of Loaded File

```
$ hadoop fs -cat /user/cloudera/test
```

```
This is a test file.
file is small
it is the sample
today is very good day
good morning everyone
file is kept in folder
```

5. Copy to Local or Get

It is used to copy file from HDFS to local file system. Here, 'test' file is present on HDFS and 'example' will be created automatically on local filesystem.

```
$ hadoop fs -copyToLocal /user/cloudera/test
example
(or)
$hadoop fs -get /user/cloudera/test example
$ ls
```

```
cloudera-manager  Desktop  Downloads  enterprise-
deployment.json  express-deployment.json  lib
parcels  Public  test  test3  workspace cm_api.py
Documents eclipse  example  kerberos  Music
```

$cat example

```
this is good
good day
have a nice day
good morning
file is kept in folder
file is small
```

6. **Moving and Copying Files Within HDFS**: to copy or move the file 'test' stored in HDFS into another directory "*Practice*" in HDFS. Enter:

```
$ hadoop fs -mv test Practice
```
(or)
```
$ hadoop fs -mv /user/cloudera/test /user/cloudera/
Practice
```

mv

Moves files from source to destination. This command allows multiple sources as well, but in this case the destination needs to be a directory. Moving files across file systems is not permitted. Here, its understood that "test" & "test1" are the two files located in HDFS default path, which will be moved to /user/cloudera/Practice.

```
$ hadoop fs -mv test test1 /user/cloudera/Practice
```

cp

Copy the files 'test', 'test1' from HDFS default location to destination. This command also allows to copy multiple sources, where the destination location must be a directory.

Options:

- *The -f option will overwrite the destination if it already exists.*

Example:

```
$ hadoop fs -cp -f test test1 /user/cloudera/
Practice
```
(or)
```
$ hadoop fs -cp -f /user/cloudera/test /user/
cloudera/test1 /user/cloudera/Practice
```

To Verify the Copied or Moved Files, Enter:

```
$ hadoop fs -ls /user/cloudera/Practice
```

```
-rw-r--r--   1 cloudera cloudera      121 2019-05-09 17:24
   /user/cloudera/Practice/test
-rw-r--r--   1 cloudera cloudera      121 2019-05-09 17:24
   /user/cloudera/Practice/test1
```

To Check the Content of Loaded File

```
$ hadoop fs -cat /user/cloudera/Practice/test
```

```
This is a test file.
file is small
it is the sample
today is very good day
good morning everyone
file is kept in folder
```

7. **Checking Disk Usage**. Another useful command to have is to figure out how much disk space we are using in HDFS. Enter:

```
$ hadoop fs -du
```

```
726   726   .Trash
121   121   Practice
0     0     sample
121   121   test
```

This command will give you an idea of how much space you are using in your HDFS home directory. Another command will show you how much space is available in HDFS across the cluster:

```
$ hadoop fs -df
```

```
Filesystem          Size      Used      Available  Use%
hdfs://quickstart.cloudera:8020 58479091712
   872710408 45221486592  1%
```

8. **appendtofile:** Append single source, or multiple sources from local file system to the destination file system. Here 'test' is the destination file to which the file 'test1' present in local filesystem will be appended.

```
Usage: hdfs dfs -appendToFile <localsrc> ...
   <dst>
```

```
$ hadoop fs -cat /user/cloudera/test
```

```
this is good
good day
have a nice day
good morning
file is kept in folder
file is small
```

```
$ hadoop fs -appendToFile test1 /user/cloudera/test
$ hadoop fs -cat /user/cloudera/test
```

```
this is good
good day
have a nice day
good morning
file is kept in folder
file is small
```

```
this is nice
nice day
have a good day
good morning
file is kept in folder
file is small
```

9. **Chmod:** Change the permissions of files. With -R, make the change recursively through the directory structure. The user must be the owner of the file, or else a super-user.

Options

- The -R option will make the change recursively through the directory structure.

```
$ hdfs dfs -chmod -R 777 /user/cloudera/Practice
(or)
$ hadoop fs -chmod -R 777 /user/cloudera/Practice
```

- To verify whether permission has been changed for the directory "Practice", Enter:

```
$hdfs dfs -ls /user/cloudera
```

```
drwxrwxrwx - cloudera cloudera 0 2019-05-09 18:53
   /user/cloudera/Practice
```

If Permission Denied, then Type the Command as Super User as Follows:

```
$ sudo su
$ hdfs dfs -chmod -R 777 /user/cloudera/Practice
```

10. Put

Copy single source or multiple sources from local file system to the destination file system. Also reads input from stdin and writes to destination file system.

To copy single file from local filesystem to HDFS

```
$ hadoop fs -put test /user/cloudera
(or)
$ hadoop fs -put /home/cloudera/test /user/cloudera
```

To check the content of loaded file

```
$ hadoop fs -cat /user/cloudera/test
```

```
This is a test file.
file is small
it is the sample
today is very good day
good morning everyone
file is kept in folder
```

To read input from stdin and writes to destination file system

```
$ hadoop fs -put - /user/cloudera/ex
```

```
today is very nice day
I finished my work
all are fine
how about u
^C
```

```
$ hadoop fs -ls /user/cloudera
```

```
-rw-r--r--   1 cloudera cloudera  67 2019-05-10 21:11
   /user/cloudera/ex._COPYING_
```

```
$ hadoop fs -cat /user/cloudera/ex._COPYING_
```

```
today is very nice day
I finished my work
all are fine
how about u
```

To copy multiple files from local filesystem to HDFS

```
hadoop fs -put test test1 test3 /user/cloudera/
Testing
```

```
$ hadoop fs -ls /user/cloudera
```

```
drwxr-xr-x   - cloudera cloudera   0 2019-05-10 21:16
   /user/cloudera/Testing
```

```
$ hadoop fs -ls /user/cloudera/Testing
```

```
Found 3 items
-rw-r--r--   1 cloudera cloudera   121 2019-05-10 21:16
    /user/cloudera/Testing/test
-rw-r--r--   1 cloudera cloudera    90 2019-05-10 21:16
    /user/cloudera/Testing/test1
-rw-r--r--   1 cloudera cloudera    88 2019-05-10 21:16
    /user/cloudera/Testing/test3
```

11. rm & rm -r

"rm" – delete the files specified as args.

"rm -r" or "rm -R" – delete the directory and sub directories & files recursively.

Option:

-skipTrash is optional and it will enable to bypass the Trash to delete the specified file(s) immediately.

-r *(or)* -R stands for recursively.

```
$hadoop fs -rm  /user/cloudera/Practice
$hadoop fs -rm -r /user/cloudera/Practice
$hadoop fs -rm -R /user/cloudera/Practice
$hadoop fs -rm -r -skipTrash /user/cloudera/Practice
```

12. count

Count the number of directories, files and bytes under the paths that match the specified file pattern. The output columns with -count are: DIR_COUNT, FILE_COUNT, CONTENT_SIZE FILE_NAME

```
$ hadoop fs -count /user/cloudera
```

```
6           7              578    /user/cloudera
```

13. **getmerge:** It takes a source directory file or files as input and concatenates files in source into the local destination file. This command concatenates files in the same directory or from multiple

directories as long as we specify their location and outputs them to the local file system, as can be seen in the Syntax below:

hadoop fs [-nl] -getmerge <src> <localdst>

hadoop fs -getmerge <src1> <src2> <localdst>

```
$hadoop fs -getmerge /user/cloudera/test /user
/cloudera/test1 /home/cloudera/sample
```

Here, two files named "test" and "test1" in HDFS are merged and stored to new file in local filesystem named "sample".

```
$ hadoop fs -getmerge -nl /user/cloudera/test
/user/cloudera/test1 /user/cloudera/Practice/test3
/home/cloudera/sample
```

Here, three files named "test" and "test1" from HDFS default location and "test3" from HDFS's "Practice directory" are merged and stored to new file in local filesystem named "sample" with a separation of new line after every file content.

14. touchz

Create a file of zero length.

```
$ hdfs dfs -touchz /user/cloudera/newfile
$ hadoop fs -ls /user/cloudera
```

```
-rw-r--r--   1 cloudera cloudera   0 2019-05-12 03:29
  /user/cloudera/newfile
```

Chapter 4

Basic Hadoop Excercises

4.1 VERIFICATION OF HADOOP CONFIGURATION FILES

1. Checking hadoop configuration files.

   a. **To verify that all services are in good health or not**

   - go to browser

   - click on "Cloud Manager"

   - enter Username: cloudera
            Password: cloudera

   - click on "login"

   - check whether required services are in green color (good health); if no, click actions button and restart

   b. **To check hadoop location**

   ```
   $cd /usr/lib/hadoop-0.20-mapreduce/
   $ls
   ```

   c. **To verify hadoop configuration files**

   ```
   [/lib/hadoop-0.20-mapreduce]$cd conf
   [/lib/hadoop-0.20-mapreduce]$ls
   $gedit core-site.xml (similarly we can open other files)
   $gedit mapred-site.xml
   $gedit yarn-site.xml
   $gedit hdfs-site.xml
   ```

NOTE!!!!

File Name	Daemon
Core-site.xml	Name node
Mapred-site.xml	Jobtracker
Master	Secondary name node
Slave	Data node
Hdfs-site.xml	Metadata file
Yarn-site.xml	Yarn-Resource manager, Yarn Scheduler
Task tracker is present along with every data node	

4.2 EXECUTION OF HADOOP MAPREDUCE PROGRAMS AND VERIFICATION OF OUTPUTS

4.2.1 Loading A File From Local File System To Hadoop File System

- **Open the terminal**
- **To verify whether all daemons are running or not**

  ```
  $ sudo jps
  ```

- *If no daemons, open cloudera manager and restart hdfs*
- **To create a folder or directory in hadoop**

  ```
  $hadoop fs -mkdir /user/cloudera/Practice
  ```

- **To verify whether or not the folder is created**

  ```
  $ hadoop fs -ls /user/cloudera
  ```

- When you open the terminal, your location is "/home/cloudera"
- **Note down the current directory location before creating the file in local system by command**

  ```
  $pwd
  ```

- **To create a file named test in local file system**

  ```
  $gedit test
  ```
  //*gedit is an editor using which a file can be read, edited etc.*

  Enter some sample data in it and then save & close

- **To verify whether or not the file is created**

```
$ls
```

- **To put or copy or move the local file into hadoop file system use any of the commands "-copyFromLocal or -put**

```
$ hadoop fs –put /home/cloudera/test   /user/
cloudera/Practice
```

- **To verify whether or not the local file is loaded into hadoop file system**

```
$hadoop fs –ls /user/cloudera/Practice
```

- **To check the content of loaded file**

```
$hadoop fs –cat /user/cloudera/Practice/test
```

To Verify the loaded file from browser

- Open the firefox browser in cloudera.

- Click the bookmark **"Hadoop"** and select **"HDFS NameNode"** from the drop down list.

- Later, click **"Utilities"** and then **"Browse the file system"** option from the drop down list. Here, one can browse through the HDFS File System. The filesystem starts from the directory root "/". Type "/" in given text box, you will see list of directories present inside the root directory.

- Click **user**

- Click **cloudera**

- Click **Practice**

- Click **test**

4.2.2 Running Various Map-Reduce Programs Available in Jar Files

- **To see the list of jar files available in hadoop**

```
$cd /usr/lib/hadoop-0.20-mapreduce/
$ls
```

- **To see the content of jar file**

```
$hadoop jar /usr/lib/hadoop-0.20-mapreduce/
hadoop-examples-2.6.0-mr1-cdh5.13.0.jar
```

(OR)

```
$hadoop jar /usr/lib/hadoop-0.20-mapreduce/
hadoop-examples-mr1.jar
```

(OR)

```
$hadoop jar /usr/lib/hadoop-0.20-mapreduce/
hadoop-examples.jar
```

TO RUN WORD COUNT PROGRAM ON LOADED FILE

EXAMPLE 1:

a. Count

b. Grep

<u>Wordcount:</u> It is used to find no: of times each word has been repeated in the given file

- Here, you need to explicitly mention a new output directory name, which will be automatically created when you run map-reduce programs.

Syntax: hadoop jar <jar file path> wordcount <input file path on hdfs> <output file path on hdfs with new output directory name>

```
$ hadoop jar /usr/lib/hadoop-0.20-mapreduce/
hadoop-examples.jar  wordcount  /user/cloudera/
Practice/test  /user/cloudera/Practice/outwc
```

- **To verify output files**

```
$hadoop fs -ls /user/cloudera/Practice

$hadoop fs -ls /user/cloudera/Practice/outwc
```

- **To see the content of output file**

```
$hadoop fs -cat /user/cloudera/Practice/outwc/
part-r-00000
```

(OR)

```
$ hadoop fs -cat /user/cloudera/Practice/
outwc/p*
```

//to see all part files content at one stretch

- **To see the output through browser**

  ```
  Click on "Hadoop→HDFS Namenode→Utilities→
  Browse the file system→/→user→cloudera →
  Practice→outwc→part-r-00000
  ```

OUTPUT:

```
a         1
day       2
file      2
folder    1
good      3
have      1
in        1
is        3
kept      1
morning   1
nice      1
small     1
this      1
```

Grep

It is used to find the no: of times a specific word or substring has been repeated in the given file

> **Syntax:** hadoop jar <jar file path> grep <input file path on hdfs> <output file path on hdfs with new output directory name> <key_word>

To run Grep program on loaded file with keyword 'file' and creating output file path.

```
$hadoop jar /usr/lib/hadoop-0.20-mapreduce/hadoop-
    examples.jar grep /user/cloudera/Practice/test /
    user/cloudera/Practice/outgrep file
```

- Here, "outgrep" is the new directory name, which will be created automatically during command execution.

- Output verification steps remain same as before.

```
OUTPUT:
2 file
```

EXAMPLE 2:

    a. WordMean

    b. WordMedian

    c. WordstandardDeviation

<u>wordmean:</u> A map/reduce program that counts the average length of the words in the input files.

> <u>Syntax:</u> **hadoop jar <jar file path> wordmean <input file path on hdfs> <output file path on hdfs with new output directory name>**

```
$hadoop jar /usr/lib/hadoop-0.20-mapreduce/hadoop-
examples.jar wordmean /user/cloudera/Practice/
test3 /user/cloudera/Practice/outmean
```

- **To verify output files**

  ```
  $ hadoop fs -ls /user/cloudera/Practice
  ```

  ```
  $ hadoop fs -ls /user/cloudera/Practice/outmean
  ```

- **To see the content of output file**

  ```
  $hadoop fs -cat /user/cloudera/Practice/
  outmean/part-r-00000
  ```

  (OR)

  ```
  $ hadoop fs -cat /user/cloudera/Practice/
  outmean/p*
  ```

- **To see the output through browser**

  ```
  Click on "Hadoop→HDFS Namenode→Utilities→
  Browse the file system→\→user→cloudera →
  Practice→outmean→part-r-00000
  ```

```
OUTPUT:
count       19
length      69
```

wordmedian: A map/reduce program that counts the median length of the words in the input files.

> **Syntax: hadoop jar <jar file path> wordmedian <input file path on hdfs> <output file path on hdfs with new output directory name>**

```
$hadoop jar /usr/lib/hadoop-0.20-mapreduce/hadoop-
examples.jar wordmedian /user/cloudera/Practice/
test3 /user/cloudera/Practice/outmedian
```

```
OUTPUT:
The median is: 4
```

wordstandarddeviation: A map/reduce program that counts the standard deviation of the length of the words in the input files.

```
$ hadoop jar /usr/lib/hadoop-0.20-mapreduce/hadoop-
examples.jar wordstandarddeviation
/user/cloudera/Practice/test3 /user/cloudera/
Practice/outstd
```

```
OUTPUT:
The standard deviation is: 1.4220269564322416
```

EXAMPLE 3:

Sudoku: A Sudoku solver.

Sudoku is a logic puzzle made up of nine 3×3 grids. Some cells in the grid have numbers, while others are blank, and the goal is to solve for the blank cell. So, the input should be a file that is in the following format:

- Nine rows of nine columns.
- Each column can contain either a number or? (which indicates a blank cell)
- Cells are separated by a space.

There is a certain way to construct Sudoku puzzles; you can't repeat a number in a column or row. So, create a sample file shown below in local Linux filesystem.

```
$gedit sud.txt
8 5 ? 3 9 ? ? ? ?
? ? 2 ? ? ? ? ? ?
? ? 6 ? 1 ? ? ? 2
? ? 4 ? ? 3 ? 5 9
? ? 8 9 ? 1 4 ? ?
3 2 ? 4 ? ? 8 ? ?
9 ? ? ? 8 ? 5 ? ?
? ? ? ? ? ? 2 ? ?
? ? ? ? 4 5 ? 7 8
```

To run the mapreduce program, enter:

```
$hadoop jar /usr/lib/hadoop-0.20-mapreduce/hadoop-
examples.jar sudoku /home/cloudera/sud.txt
```

Note!!! The input file has to be on local filesystem and need not to be copied to HDFS

```
Solving /home/cloudera/sud.txt
8 5 1 3 9 2 6 4 7
4 3 2 6 7 8 1 9 5
7 9 6 5 1 4 3 8 2
6 1 4 8 2 3 7 5 9
5 7 8 9 6 1 4 2 3
3 2 9 4 5 7 8 1 6
9 4 7 2 8 6 5 3 1
1 8 5 7 3 9 2 6 4
2 6 3 1 4 5 9 7 8
Found 1 solutions
```

EXAMPLE 4:

Pi (π):

The pi sample uses a statistical (quasi-Monte Carlo) method to estimate the value of pi. Points are placed at random in a unit square. The square also contains a circle. The probability that the points fall within the circle are equal to the area of the circle, pi/4. The value of pi can be estimated from the value of 4R. R is the ratio of the number of points that are inside the circle to the total number of points that are within the square. The larger the sample of points used, the better the estimate is.

Use the following command to run this sample. This command uses 16 maps with 10,000,000 samples each to estimate the value of pi:

```
$hadoop jar /usr/lib/hadoop-0.20-mapreduce/hadoop-
examples.jar pi 16 10000000
```

```
OUTPUT:
Estimated value of Pi is 3.14159155000000000000
```

EXAMPLE 5:

    a. randomtextwriter

    b. randomwriter

randomtextwriter: A map/reduce program that writes 10GB of random textual data per node.

```
$hadoop jar /usr/lib/hadoop-0.20-mapreduce/hadoop-
examples.jar randomtextwriter /user/cloudera/
rantext
```

After execution of the program you can find that a directory named "rantext" is newly created which contains the output of the randomtextwriter program. We can find that the newly created directory contains 11 files. one of the 11 files name SUCCESS, which tells that the program has run successfully and another 10 files are written by the random writer. Each of the 10 files are of size 1 gb (approx).

- **To verify output files**

```
$ hadoop fs -ls /user/cloudera/rantext
```

- **To see the content of output file**

```
$hadoop fs -cat /user/cloudera/rantext/
part-m-00000
```

(OR)

```
$ hadoop fs -cat /user/rantext/outmean/p*
```

- ## To see the output through browser

```
Click on "Hadoop→HDFS Namenode→Utilities→
Browse the file system→\→user→
cloudera →rantext →part-m-00000
```

Browse Directory

/user/cloudera/rantext
Go!

Permission	Owner	Group	Size	Last Modified	Replication	Block Size	Name
-rw-r--r--	cloudera	cloudera	0 B	Tue May 14 21:46:04 -0700 2019	1	128 MB	_SUCCESS
-rw-r--r--	cloudera	cloudera	1.03 GB	Tue May 14 21:42:07 -0700 2019	1	128 MB	part-m-00000
-rw-r--r--	cloudera	cloudera	1.03 GB	Tue May 14 21:42:07 -0700 2019	1	128 MB	part-m-00001
-rw-r--r--	cloudera	cloudera	1.03 GB	Tue May 14 21:43:14 -0700 2019	1	128 MB	part-m-00002
-rw-r--r--	cloudera	cloudera	1.03 GB	Tue May 14 21:43:16 -0700 2019	1	128 MB	part-m-00003
-rw-r--r--	cloudera	cloudera	1.03 GB	Tue May 14 21:44:07 -0700 2019	1	128 MB	part-m-00004
-rw-r--r--	cloudera	cloudera	1.03 GB	Tue May 14 21:44:09 -0700 2019	1	128 MB	part-m-00005
-rw-r--r--	cloudera	cloudera	1.03 GB	Tue May 14 21:45:04 -0700 2019	1	128 MB	part-m-00006
-rw-r--r--	cloudera	cloudera	1.03 GB	Tue May 14 21:45:04 -0700 2019	1	128 MB	part-m-00007
-rw-r--r--	cloudera	cloudera	1.03 GB	Tue May 14 21:46:03 -0700 2019	1	128 MB	part-m-00008
-rw-r--r--	cloudera	cloudera	1.03 GB	Tue May 14 21:46:04 -0700 2019	1	128 MB	part-m-00009

randomwriter: A map/reduce program that writes 10GB (by default) of random data per node.

Each map takes a single file name as input and writes random BytesWritable keys and values to the DFS sequence file. The maps do not emit any output and the reduce phase is not used.

The specifics of the generated data are configurable. The configuration variables are:

Name	Default Value	Description
test.randomwriter.maps_per_host	10	Number of maps/host
test.randomwrite.bytes_per_map	1073741824	Number of bytes written/map
test.randomwrite.min_key	10	minimum size of the key in bytes
test.randomwrite.max_key	1000	maximum size of the key in bytes

Name	Default Value	Description
test.randomwrite.min_value	0	minimum size of the value
test.randomwrite.max_value	20000	maximum size of the value

- **To generate random data of 10 GB with default configuration, Enter:**

```
$hadoop jar /usr/lib/hadoop-0.20-mapreduce/
hadoop-examples.jar randomtextwriter /user/
cloudera/randefault
```

- **To produce smaller size file (each approx. 1KB) with 5 mappers, min_key_as 1 and max_key as 10, min_value as 0 and max_value as 1000; Enter as follows:**

```
$hadoop jar /usr/lib/hadoop-0.20-
mapreduce/hadoop-examples.jar randomwriter
-Dmapreduce.randomwriter.bytespermap=1000
-Dmapreduce.randomwriter.mapsperhost=5
-Dmapreduce.randomwriter.minkey=1
-Dmapreduce.randomwriter.maxkey=10
-Dmapreduce.randomwriter.minvalue=0
-Dmapreduce.randomwriter.maxvalue=1000 /user/
cloudera/randwr
```

- **To verify output files**

```
$ hadoop fs -ls /user/cloudera/randwr
```

- **To see the content of output file**

```
$hadoop fs -cat /user/cloudera/randwr/
part-m-00000
```

(OR)

```
$ hadoop fs -cat /user/randwr/p*
```

- **To see the output through browser**

  ```
  Click on "Hadoop→HDFS Namenode→Utilities→
  Browse the file system→\→user→cloudera→
  randwr→part-m-00000
  ```

Browse Directory

/user/cloudera/randwr   Go!

Permission	Owner	Group	Size	Last Modified	Replication	Block Size	Name
-rw-r--r--	cloudera	cloudera	0 B	Wed May 15 18:54:12 -0700 2019	1	128 MB	_SUCCESS
-rw-r--r--	cloudera	cloudera	1.29 KB	Wed May 15 18:53:58 -0700 2019	1	128 MB	part-m-00000
-rw-r--r--	cloudera	cloudera	1.45 KB	Wed May 15 18:53:58 -0700 2019	1	128 MB	part-m-00001
-rw-r--r--	cloudera	cloudera	1.27 KB	Wed May 15 18:54:05 -0700 2019	1	128 MB	part-m-00002
-rw-r--r--	cloudera	cloudera	1.37 KB	Wed May 15 18:54:08 -0700 2019	1	128 MB	part-m-00003
-rw-r--r--	cloudera	cloudera	1.39 KB	Wed May 15 18:54:11 -0700 2019	1	128 MB	part-m-00004

EXAMPLE 6:

a. Teragen

b. Terasort

c. Teravalidate

TeraGen: A MapReduce program that generates rows of data to sort.

TeraSort: Samples the input data and uses MapReduce to sort the data into a total order. TeraSort is a standard MapReduce sort, except for a custom partitioner. The partitioner uses a sorted list of N-1 sampled keys that define the key range for each reduce. In particular, all keys such that sample[i-1] <= key < sample[i] are sent to reduce i. This partitioner guarantees that the outputs of reduce i are all less than the output of reduce i+1.

TeraValidate: A MapReduce program that validates that the output is globally sorted. It creates one map per file in the output directory, and each map ensures that each key is less than or equal to the previous one. The map function generates records of the first and last keys of each file. The reduce function ensures that the first key of file i is greater than the last key of file i-1. Any problems are reported as an output of the reduce phase, with the keys that are out of order.

Use the following steps to generate data, sort, and then validate the output:

Step 1: Generate 10 KB of data (in the below command each map task generates 1KB) in storage location "/user/cloudera/terainput" as sequence files.

```
$ hadoop jar /usr/lib/hadoop-0.20-mapreduce/hadoop-
examples.jar teragen -Dmapred.map.tasks=10 10000
/user/cloudera/terainput
```

The -Dmapred.map.tasks tells Hadoop how many map tasks to use for this job. The final two parameters instruct the job to create 10 KB of data and to store it at /user/cloudera/terainput.

- **To verify output files**

  ```
  $ hadoop fs -ls /user/cloudera/terainput
  ```

- **To see the content of output file**

  ```
  $hadoop fs -cat /user/cloudera/terainput/
  part-m-00000
  ```

  (OR)

  ```
  $ hadoop fs -cat /user/terainput /p*
  ```

- **To see the output through browser**

  ```
  Click on "Hadoop→HDFS Namenode→Utilities→
  Browse the file system→\→user→cloudera→
  terainput →part-m-00000
  ```

OUTPUT:

/user/cloudera/terainput   Go!

Permission	Owner	Group	Size	Last Modified	Replication	Block Size	Name
-rw-r--r--	cloudera	cloudera	0 B	Thu May 16 03:55:48 -0700 2019	1	128 MB	_SUCCESS
-rw-r--r--	cloudera	cloudera	97.66 KB	Thu May 16 03:55:14 -0700 2019	1	128 MB	part-m-00000
-rw-r--r--	cloudera	cloudera	97.66 KB	Thu May 16 03:55:15 -0700 2019	1	128 MB	part-m-00001
-rw-r--r--	cloudera	cloudera	97.66 KB	Thu May 16 03:55:23 -0700 2019	1	128 MB	part-m-00002
-rw-r--r--	cloudera	cloudera	97.66 KB	Thu May 16 03:55:23 -0700 2019	1	128 MB	part-m-00003
-rw-r--r--	cloudera	cloudera	97.66 KB	Thu May 16 03:55:32 -0700 2019	1	128 MB	part-m-00004
-rw-r--r--	cloudera	cloudera	97.66 KB	Thu May 16 03:55:31 -0700 2019	1	128 MB	part-m-00005
-rw-r--r--	cloudera	cloudera	97.66 KB	Thu May 16 03:55:39 -0700 2019	1	128 MB	part-m-00006
-rw-r--r--	cloudera	cloudera	97.66 KB	Thu May 16 03:55:39 -0700 2019	1	128 MB	part-m-00007
-rw-r--r--	cloudera	cloudera	97.66 KB	Thu May 16 03:55:47 -0700 2019	1	128 MB	part-m-00008
-rw-r--r--	cloudera	cloudera	97.66 KB	Thu May 16 03:55:48 -0700 2019	1	128 MB	part-m-00009

Step 2: Use the following command to sort the data:

```
$ hadoop jar /usr/lib/hadoop-0.20-mapreduce/
hadoop-examples.jar terasort -Dmapred.map.tasks=10
-Dmapred.reduce.tasks=5 /user/cloudera/terainput
/user/cloudera/terasortop
```

The `-Dmapred.reduce.tasks` tells Hadoop how many reduce tasks to use for the job. The final two parameters are just the input and output locations for data.

***Use the same steps shown before for verification of output through browser and terminal.**

OUTPUT:

Browse Directory

/user/cloudera/terasortop   Go!

Permission	Owner	Group	Size	Last Modified	Replication	Block Size	Name
-rw-r--r--	cloudera	cloudera	0 B	Thu May 16 04:04:09 -0700 2019	1	128 MB	_SUCCESS
-rw-r--r--	cloudera	cloudera	44 B	Thu May 16 04:00:57 -0700 2019	10	128 MB	_partition.lst
-rw-r--r--	cloudera	cloudera	195.31 KB	Thu May 16 04:03:31 -0700 2019	1	128 MB	part-r-00000
-rw-r--r--	cloudera	cloudera	195.31 KB	Thu May 16 04:03:31 -0700 2019	1	128 MB	part-r-00001
-rw-r--r--	cloudera	cloudera	195.31 KB	Thu May 16 04:03:54 -0700 2019	1	128 MB	part-r-00002
-rw-r--r--	cloudera	cloudera	195.31 KB	Thu May 16 04:03:57 -0700 2019	1	128 MB	part-r-00003
-rw-r--r--	cloudera	cloudera	195.31 KB	Thu May 16 04:04:09 -0700 2019	1	128 MB	part-r-00004

Step 3: Use the following to validate the data generated by the sort:

```
$ hadoop jar /usr/lib/hadoop-0.20-mapreduce/hadoop-
examples.jar teravalidate -Dmapred.map.tasks=10
-Dmapred.reduce.tasks=5 /user/cloudera/terasortop
/user/cloudera/teravalidate
```

5 Hands-On with Sqoop

Sqoop is a tool designed to transfer data between Hadoop and relational database servers. It is used to import data from relational databases such as MySQL, Oracle to Hadoop HDFS, and export from Hadoop file system to relational databases. It is provided by the Apache Software Foundation.

Reduce phase is required in case of aggregations. But Apache Sqoop just imports and exports the data; it does not perform any aggregations. Map job launch multiple mappers depending on the number defined by the user. For Sqoop import, each mapper task will be assigned with a part of data to be imported. Sqoop distributes the input data among the mappers equally to get high performance. Then each mapper creates a connection with the database using JDBC and fetches the part of data assigned by Sqoop and writes it into HDFS.

5.1 VERIFYING SQOOP STATUS THROUGH CLOUDERA MANAGER AND CREATE DATABASE AND USER ACCOUNT IN MYSQL

For SQOOP

- Open the browser of VM and select "Cloudera Manager"

- Login: cloudera

- Password: cloudera

- Check whether or not SQOOP is in good helath

- If no, then restart the SQOOP in "actions" button

For Mysql

- **open the terminal**
- **To start mysql services**

  ```
  $sudo service mysqld start
  ```

- **To connect to mysql as root login**

  ```
  $mysql -u root -p
  ```

  Password: cloudera

  1. **To create Database**

     ```
     mysql>create database lab
     ```

     - *To show the existing data bases*

     ```
     mysql>show databases;
     ```

  2. **To create your own account**

     ```
     mysql>create user nh001 identified by "1234";
     ```

     - *To show the existing users*

  ```
  mysql>select user from mysql.user;
  ```

  3. **To grant permission to the user for creating tables on that database**

     ```
     mysql>grant all on lab.* to "nh001";
     ```

     - **Exit**

     ```
     mysql>quit
     ```

NOTE!!! If you don't want to create your own user account then you can continue with username "root" and password as "cloudera" i,e. ignore step no:2 and step no:3

Steps to be followed after login to your account

To login with your account

```
$mysql -u nh001 -p
```

Password: 1234

1. **To verify the database names**

   ```
   mysql>show databases;
   ```

2. **To choose the database you want to use**

   ```
   mysql>use lab;
   ```

3. **To create tables**

   ```
   mysql>create table emp(empno int primary
   key,ename varchar(10),age int);
   ```

   ```
   mysql>create table dept(dno int primary
   key,dname varchar(5));
   ```

4. **To insert records into the tables**

   ```
   mysql>insert into emp values(1001,'ram',21),
   (1002,'sita',22),(1003,'ravi',23),
   (1004,'teja',21),(1005,'meena',22),
   (1006,'mona',20),(1007,'sona',21),
   (1008,'harish',23),(1009,'james',35),
   (1010,'jacob',30);
   ```

   ```
   mysql>insert into dept values(10,'cse'),
   (20,'ise'),(30,'me'),(40,'mba'),(50,'mca'),
   (60,'au'),(70,'civil'),(80,'ece'),(90,'eee');
   ```

- **Exit**

5.2 SQOOP BASIC COMMANDS

```
Syntax:
$sqoop <tool-name> <tool-arguments>
These tool-arguments starts with "--" and followed
by its value
```

> **NOTE!!!**
>
> *** There is no space between -- and tool-arguments. It's a single word like
> --connect, --table, --query.
>
> *** But there is a space between tool-argument and its value.

a. To List-Databases

The following command is used to list all the databases in the MySQL database server.

```
$sqoop list-databases --connect "jdbc:mysql:
//localhost"  --username nh001 --password  1234
```

```
OUTPUT:
information_schema
lab
```

Sqoop is designed to import tables from a database into HDFS. To do so, you must specify a connect string that describes how to connect to the database. The connect string is similar to a URL, and is communicated to Sqoop with the --connect argument.

You can use the --username and --password or -P parameters to supply a username and a password to the database.

b. To List the Tables

The following command is used to list all the tables in the **lab** database of MySQL database server.

```
$sqoop list-tables  --connect "jdbc:mysql:
//localhost/lab"   --username nh001
--password 1234
```

```
OUTPUT:
dept
emp
```

c. To Run sql Queries from Hadoop Using Eval

- Using eval tool, we can evaluate any type of SQL query and display the result on to the console.

- Sqoop eval tool can be applicable for both modeling and defining the SQL statements. That means, we can use eval for insert statements too. If the command executes successfully, then it will display the status of the updated rows on the console.

```
$sqoop eval --connect "jdbc:mysql:
//localhost/lab"          --username nh001
--password 1234 --query "select * from dept"
```

OUTPUT:
```
---------------
| dno    | dname |
---------------

| 10     | cse    |
| 20     | ise    |
| 30     | me     |
| 40     | mba    |
| 50     | mca    |
| 60     | au     |
| 70     | civil  |
| 80     | ece    |
| 90     | eee    |
```

```
$sqoop eval --connect "jdbc:mysql://localhost/lab"
--username nh001 --password 1234 --query "select
count(*) from dept "
```

OUTPUT:
```
-----------------------------
| count (*)                  |
-----------------------------
| 9                          |
```

```
$sqoop eval --connect "jdbc:mysql://localhost/lab"
--username nh001 --password 1234 --query "select
dname from dept where dno>50"
```

OUTPUT:
```
---------
| dname |
---------
| au     |
```

```
| civil  |
| ece    |
| eee    |
```

Exercise: Perform Insert, Update, Delete operation also through eval tool.

```
$ sqoop eval --connect "jdbc:mysql://localhost/lab"
--username nh001 --password 1234 --query "insert
into dept values(100,'bt')"
```

```
$ sqoop eval --connect "jdbc:mysql://localhost/lab"
--username nh001 --password 1234 --query "update
dept set dname='bio' where dno=100"
```

```
$ sqoop eval --connect "jdbc:mysql://localhost/lab"
--username nh001 --password 1234 --query "delete
from dept where dname='bio'"
```

> **Note!!!** Verify the changes made in database using Sqoop tool either by
>
> - taking another terminal
> - log into MySQL
> - verify table content
>   (OR)
> - use eval sub-command itself using the query "select * from dept"

5.3 IMPORT OF TABLES FROM MYSQL DATABASE TO HDFS

- Import of all tables to default directory and specific directory.
- Import of specific tables to default directory and target directory.
- Import of subset of tables using 'where' clause to default and specific directory.
- Import as sequence file.
- Incremental import.

5.3.1 Import-all-tables to Default Directory

- The import-all-tables tool imports all tables from database "lab" to HDFS. Data from each table is stored in a separate directory in HDFS.

- Each table must have a single-column primary key or **-m 1** option must be used (to make no: of mappers as one).

NOTE!!! Here -m 1 specifies one mapper for each table. All the tables are downloaded in default directory. The default number of mappers used is 4. You can change this by appending the command by "-m number_of_mappers".

```
$sqoop import-all-tables —connect
"jdbc:mysql://localhost/lab" --username nh001
--password   1234
```

To check whether or not tables are imported

```
$hadoop fs -ls /user/cloudera
```

```
OUTPUT:
drwxr-xr-x - cloudera cloudera 0 2018-01-30 22:41 /user/cloudera/dept
drwxr-xr-x - cloudera cloudera 0 2018-01-30 22:42 /user/cloudera/emp
```

To check for a particular table

```
$hadoop fs -ls /user/cloudera/dept
```

```
OUTPUT:
-rw-r--r-- 3 cloudera cloudera  0 2018-01-30 22:41
   /user/cloudera/dept/_SUCCESS
drwxr-xr-x - cloudera cloudera 0 2018-01-30 22:40
   /user/cloudera/dept/_logs
-rw-r--r-- 3 cloudera cloudera 20 2018-01-30 22:41
   /user/cloudera/dept/part-m-00000
-rw-r--r-- 3 cloudera cloudera 14 2018-01-30 22:41
   /user/cloudera/dept/part-m-00001
-rw-r--r-- 3 cloudera cloudera 15 2018-01-30 22:41
   /user/cloudera/dept/part-m-00002
-rw-r--r-- 3 cloudera cloudera 21 2018-01-30 22:41
   /user/cloudera/dept/part-m-00003
```

To see the records of MySQL table on HDFS file

> **NOTE!!!** All the following Sqoop command outputs in HDFS (in this chapter) can be verified through browser also by following the link for the respective directories:
>
> ```
> Click on "Hadoop→HDFS Namenode→Utilities→
> Browse the file system→\→user→cloudera→
> dept→part-m-00000
> ```
>
> **(OR)**
>
> Verify through terminal as shown in every sub-section

```
$hadoop fs -cat /user/cloudera/dept/part-m-00000
```

```
OUTPUT:
10,cse
20,ise
30,me
```

```
$hadoop fs -cat /user/cloudera/dept/part-m-00001
```

```
OUTPUT:
40,mba
50,mca
```

```
$hadoop fs -cat /user/cloudera/dept/part-m-00002
```

```
OUTPUT:
60,au
70,civil
```

```
$hadoop fs -cat /user/cloudera/dept/part-m-00003
```

```
OUTPUT:
80,ece
90,eee
100,bt
```

(OR)

```
$hadoop fs -cat /user/cloudera/dept/part*
```

```
OUTPUT:
10,cse
20,ise
30,me
40,mba
50,mca
60,au
70,civil
80,ece
90,eee
100,bt
```

5.3.1.1 Import-all-tables to a specific directory

To import MySQL all tables to the specific directory "sample"

```
$sqoop import-all-tables --connect    "jdbc:mysql://
localhost/lab" --username nh001 --password  1234
--warehouse-dir /user/cloudera/sample
```

> **Note!!!** Here, "sample" directory is automatically created if it doesn't exists or a new empty "sample" directory can be created before execution of command.
>
> I,e. we can adjust the parent directory of the import with the `--warehouse-dir` argument

To check whether or not tables are imported

```
$hadoop fs -ls /user/cloudera/sample
```

```
OUTPUT:
drwxr-xr-x  - cloudera cloudera  0 2018-01-30 22:59
    /user/cloudera/sample/dept
drwxr-xr-x  - cloudera cloudera  0 2018-01-30 22:59
    /user/cloudera/sample/emp
```

To check for a particular table

```
$hadoop fs -ls /user/cloudera/sample/dept
```

```
OUTPUT:
-rw-r--r--   3 cloudera cloudera   0 2018-01-30 22:59
   /user/cloudera/sample/dept/_SUCCESS
drwxr-xr-x  - cloudera cloudera   0 2018-01-30 22:58
   /user/cloudera/sample/dept/_logs
-rw-r--r--   3 cloudera cloudera  20 2018-01-30 22:59
   /user/cloudera/sample/dept/part-m-00000
-rw-r--r--   3 cloudera cloudera  14 2018-01-30 22:59
   /user/cloudera/sample/dept/part-m-00001
-rw-r--r--   3 cloudera cloudera  15 2018-01-30 22:59
   /user/cloudera/sample/dept/part-m-00002
-rw-r--r--   3 cloudera cloudera  21 2018-01-30 22:59
   /user/cloudera/sample/dept/part-m-00003
```

```
$hadoop fs -ls /user/cloudera/sample/emp
```

```
OUTPUT:
-rw-r--r--   3 cloudera cloudera   0 2018-01-30 22:59
   /user/cloudera/sample/emp/_SUCCESS
drwxr-xr-x  - cloudera cloudera   0 2018-01-30 22:59
   /user/cloudera/sample/emp/_logs
-rw-r--r--   3 cloudera cloudera  38 2018-01-30 22:59
   /user/cloudera/sample/emp/part-m-00000
-rw-r--r--   3 cloudera cloudera  27 2018-01-30 22:59
   /user/cloudera/sample/emp/part-m-00001
-rw-r--r--   3 cloudera cloudera  26 2018-01-30 22:59
   /user/cloudera/sample/emp/part-m-00002
-rw-r--r--   3 cloudera cloudera  43 2018-01-30 22:59
   /user/cloudera/sample/emp/part-m-00003
```

To see the records of MySQL table on HDFS file

```
$hadoop fs -cat /user/cloudera/sample/emp/part*
```

```
OUTPUT:
1001,ram,21
1002,sita,22
1003,ravi,23
1004,teja,21
1005,meena,22
1006,mona,20
1007,sona,21
1008,harish,23
1009,james,35
1010,jacob,30
```

5.3.1.2 Import-all-tables to specific directory with only one mapper (*-m stands for no:of mappers*)

To remove already existing tables in the current directory

```
$hadoop fs -rm -R /user/cloudera/sample/*

$sqoop import-all-tables --connect "jdbc:mysql:
//localhost/lab" --username nh001 --password   1234
--warehouse-dir /user/cloudera/sample -m 1
```

To check whether or not tables are imported

```
$hadoop fs -ls /user/cloudera/sample/
```

```
OUTPUT:
drwxr-xr-x  - cloudera cloudera  0 2018-01-30 23:08
    /user/cloudera/sample/dept
drwxr-xr-x  - cloudera cloudera  0 2018-01-30 23:08
    /user/cloudera/sample/emp
```

To check for a particular table

```
$hadoop fs -ls /user/cloudera/sample/emp
```

```
OUTPUT:
-rw-r--r--   3 cloudera cloudera    0 2018-01-30 23:08
   /user/cloudera/sample/emp/_SUCCESS
drwxr-xr-x  - cloudera cloudera    0 2018-01-30 23:08
   /user/cloudera/sample/emp/_logs
-rw-r--r--   3 cloudera cloudera 134 2018-01-30 23:08
   /user/cloudera/sample/emp/part-m-00000
```

To see the records of MySQL table on HDFS file

```
$hadoop fs -cat /user/cloudera/sample/emp/
part-m-00000
```

```
OUTPUT:
1001,ram,21
1002,sita,22
1003,ravi,23
1004,teja,21
1005,meena,22
1006,mona,20
1007,sona,21
1008,harish,23
1009,james,35
1010,jacob,30
```

5.3.2 Import of Specific Table to Default Directory of HDFS

Sqoop tool 'import' is used to import table data from a single MySQL table to the Hadoop file system as a text file.

Argument:

--table `<table-name>`	The table to be imported from MySQL

To remove MySQL table's same name file from default directory (to avoid file already exists error)

```
$hadoop fs -rm -R /user/cloudera/*
```

To perform single table import to default directory

```
$sqoop import --connect "jdbc:mysql:
//localhost/lab"            --username nh001
--password 1234 --table dept
```

To check whether or not tables are imported

```
$hadoop fs -ls /user/cloudera/
```

```
OUTPUT:
drwxr-xr-x   - cloudera cloudera  0 2018-01-30 23:15
   /user/cloudera/dept
drwxr-xr-x   - cloudera cloudera  0 2018-01-30 22:54
   /user/cloudera/sample
```

To check for a particular table

```
$hadoop fs -ls /user/cloudera/dept
```

```
OUTPUT:
-rw-r--r--  3 cloudera cloudera   0 2018-01-30 23:15
   /user/cloudera/dept/_SUCCESS
drwxr-xr-x  - cloudera cloudera   0 2018-01-30 23:14
   /user/cloudera/dept/_logs
-rw-r--r--  3 cloudera cloudera  20 2018-01-30 23:15
   /user/cloudera/dept/part-m-00000
-rw-r--r--  3 cloudera cloudera  14 2018-01-30 23:15
   /user/cloudera/dept/part-m-00001
-rw-r--r--  3 cloudera cloudera  15 2018-01-30 23:15
   /user/cloudera/dept/part-m-00002
-rw-r--r--  3 cloudera cloudera  21 2018-01-30 23:15
   /user/cloudera/dept/part-m-00003
```

To see the records of mysql table on hdfs file

```
$hadoop fs -cat /user/cloudera/dept/part*
```

```
OUTPUT:
10,cse
20,ise
30,me
40,mba
```

```
50,mca
60,au
70,civil
80,ece
90,eee
100,bt
```

5.3.2.1 Import of specific table from Mysql to a target directory of hdfs

We can specify the target directory while importing table data into HDFS using the Sqoop import tool. Following is the syntax to specify the target directory as option to the Sqoop import command.

```
--target-dir <new or existing directory>
```

```
$sqoop import --connect "jdbc:mysql://localhost/lab"
--username nh001 --password 1234 --table dept
--target-dir  /user/cloudera/dnew
```

To check whether or not tables are imported

```
$hadoop fs -ls /user/cloudera
```

```
OUTPUT:

drwxr-xr-x  -cloudera  cloudera 0 2018-01-30 23:21
/user/cloudera/dnew
```

To check for a particular table

```
$hadoop fs -ls /user/cloudera/dnew
```

```
OUTPUT:
-rw-r--r--  3 cloudera cloudera   0 2018-01-30 23:21
    /user/cloudera/dnew/_SUCCESS
drwxr-xr-x  - cloudera cloudera   0 2018-01-30 23:20
    /user/cloudera/dnew/_logs
-rw-r--r--  3 cloudera cloudera  20 2018-01-30 23:21
    /user/cloudera/dnew/part-m-00000
-rw-r--r--  3 cloudera cloudera  14 2018-01-30 23:21
    /user/cloudera/dnew/part-m-00001
```

```
-rw-r--r--   3 cloudera cloudera   15 2018-01-30 23:21
   /user/cloudera/dnew/part-m-00002
-rw-r--r--   3 cloudera cloudera   21 2018-01-30 23:21
   /user/cloudera/dnew/part-m-00003
```

To see the records of mysql table on hdfs file

```
$hadoop fs -cat /user/dnew/part*
```

```
OUTPUT:
10,cse
20,ise
30,me
40,mba
50,mca
60,au
70,civil
80,ece
90,eee
100,bt
```

NOTE!!

--warehouse-dir, --target-dir: is used when you want to import MySQL data to a different directory path other than default directory (say ex: **/user/cloudera/dnew**)

For --warehouse-dir:

Automatically, a new directory is created with same name as MySQL table (ex: MySQL table in **lab** database is **emp**, so after doing import; a new directory **emp** will be created inside your given path I,e **/user/ cloudera/dnew**)

For --target-dir:

You are given a choice to mention your own directory name where data from MySQL will be imported. I,e say MySQL table name is **emp in lab** database and if you mention **--target-dir /user/cloudera/dnew**; then emp data will be directly imported by creating a new directory named **'dnew'** and data will be inside that directory.

5.3.3 Import subset of data from mysql to hdfs [optional -m 1]

We can import a subset of a table using the 'where' clause in Sqoop import tool. It executes the corresponding SQL query in the respective database server and stores the result in a target directory in HDFS.

The syntax for where clause is as follows.

```
--where    <condition>
```

```
$sqoop import --connect "jdbc:mysql://localhost/lab"
--username nh001 --password 1234 --table dept
--where "dno>'50'" --target-dir /user/cloudera/
deptsubset
```

To check whether or not tables are imported

```
$hadoop fs -ls /user/cloudera
```

```
OUTPUT:
drwxr-xr-x  - cloudera cloudera   0 2018-01-30 23:35
   /user/cloudera/deptsubset
```

To check contents of newly created directory

```
$hadoop fs -ls /user/cloudera/deptsubset
```

```
OUTPUT:
-rw-r--r--  3 cloudera cloudera   0 2018-01-30 23:35
   /user/cloudera/deptsubset/_SUCCESS
drwxr-xr-x  - cloudera cloudera   0 2018-01-30 23:35
   /user/cloudera/deptsubset/_logs
-rw-r--r--  3 cloudera cloudera   6 2018-01-30 23:35
   /user/cloudera/deptsubset/part-m-00000
-rw-r--r--  3 cloudera cloudera   9 2018-01-30 23:35
   /user/cloudera/deptsubset/part-m-00001
-rw-r--r--  3 cloudera cloudera   7 2018-01-30 23:35
   /user/cloudera/deptsubset/part-m-00002
-rw-r--r--  3 cloudera cloudera  14 2018-01-30 23:35
   /user/cloudera/deptsubset/part-m-00003
```

To see the subset records of Mysql table on hdfs file

```
$hadoop fs -cat /user/cloudera/deptsubset/part*
```

```
OUTPUT:
60,au
70,civil
80,ece
90,eee
100,bt
```

5.3.4 Import specific columns of a MySQL table to hdfs[*optional -m 1*]

You can select a subset of columns and control their ordering by using the --columns argument. This should include a comma-delimited list of columns to import.

The syntax for where clause is as follows.

```
--columns <"list of columns separated by comma">
```

```
$sqoop import --connect "jdbc:mysql://localhost/lab"
--username nh001 --password 1234 --table emp --columns
"ename,age" --target-dir /user/cloudera/col
```

To check whether or not table is imported

```
$hadoop fs -ls /user/cloudera
```

```
OUTPUT:
drwxr-xr-x   - cloudera cloudera  0 2019-05-17 22:28
   /user/cloudera/col
```

To check content of newly created directory

```
$ hadoop fs -ls /user/cloudera/col
```

```
OUTPUT:
-rw-r--r-- 1 cloudera cloudera   0 2019-05-17 22:28
   /user/cloudera/col/_SUCCESS
-rw-r--r-- 1 cloudera cloudera  23 2019-05-17 22:28
   /user/cloudera/col/part-m-00000
```

```
-rw-r--r--   1 cloudera cloudera   17 2019-05-17 22:28
   /user/cloudera/col/part-m-00001
-rw-r--r--   1 cloudera cloudera   16 2019-05-17 22:28
   /user/cloudera/col/part-m-00002
-rw-r--r--   1 cloudera cloudera   28 2019-05-17 22:28
   /user/cloudera/col/part-m-00003
```

To see the records of Mysql table on hdfs file

```
$hadoop fs -cat /user/cloudera/col/part*
```

```
OUTPUT:
ram,21
sita,22
ravi,23
teja,21
meena,22
mona,20
sona,21
harish,23
james,35
jacob,30
```

5.3.5 Import of a Mysql table as sequence file or avro data file

SQOOP allows to store Mysql tables in different file format as plain text file (by default), sequence file, avro data file.

5.3.5.1 Sequence File

SequenceFiles are a binary format that store individual records in custom record-specific data types. These data types are manifested as Java classes. Sqoop will automatically generate these data types for you. This format supports exact storage of all data in binary representations, and is appropriate for storing binary data. The command to import Mysql table data as sequence file on hdfs is:

Syntax: --as-sequencefile
Here, -m 1 argument is optional. If not mentioned, then by default 4 mappers will be considered.

```
$sqoop import --connect "jdbc:mysql://localhost/lab"
--username nh001 --password 1234 --table dept --target-
dir /user/cloudera/deptseq --as-sequencefile -m 1
```

To check whether or not tables are imported

```
$hadoop fs -ls /user/cloudera/
```

> **OUTPUT:**
> *drwxr-xr-x   - cloudera cloudera   0 2018-01-30 23:35*
>   */user/cloudera/deptseq*

To check for a particular table

```
$hadoop fs -ls /user/cloudera/deptseq
```

> **OUTPUT:**
> *-rw-r--r--   3 cloudera cloudera   0 2018-01-30 23:35*
>   */user/cloudera/deptseq /_SUCCESS*
> *drwxr-xr-x   - cloudera cloudera   0 2018-01-30 23:35*
>   */user/cloudera/deptseq /_logs*
> *-rw-r--r--   3 cloudera cloudera   6 2018-01-30 23:35*
>   */user/cloudera/deptseq/part-m-00000*

To see the records of Mysql table on hdfs file

```
$hadoop fs -cat /user/cloudera/deptseq/part*
```

5.3.5.2 Avro datafiles

Avro datafiles are a compact, efficient binary format that provides interoperability with applications written in other programming languages. The command to import Mysql table data as avro dat file on hdfs is:

> **Syntax: --as-avrodatafile**
>
> Here, -m 1 argument is optional. If not mentioned, then by default 4 mappers will be considered.

```
$sqoop import --connect "jdbc:mysql://localhost/lab"
--username nh001 --password 1234 --table dept --target-
dir /user/cloudera/deptavro --as-avrodatafile -m 1
```

To check whether or not tables are imported

```
$hadoop fs -ls /user/cloudera/
```

> **OUTPUT:**
> ```
> drwxr-xr-x   - cloudera cloudera  0 2018-01-30 23:38
>    /user/cloudera/deptavro
> ```

To check the contents of newly created directory

```
$hadoop fs -ls /user/cloudera/deptseq
```

> **OUTPUT:**
> ```
> -rw-r--r--   3 cloudera cloudera  0 2018-01-30 23:38
>    /user/cloudera/deptavro/_SUCCESS
> drwxr-xr-x   - cloudera cloudera  0 2018-01-30 23:38
>    /user/cloudera/deptavro/_logs
> -rw-r--r--   3 cloudera cloudera  6 2018-01-30 23:38
>    /user/cloudera/deptavro/part-m-00000
> ```

To see the records of Mysql table on hdfs file

```
$hadoop fs -cat /user/cloudera/deptavro/part*
```

> **Controlling Parallelism**
>
> When performing parallel imports, Sqoop needs a criterion by which it can split the workload. Sqoop uses a *splitting column* to split the workload. By default, Sqoop will identify the primary key column (if present) in a table and use it as the splitting column. The low and high values for the splitting column are retrieved from the database, and the map tasks operate on evenly-sized components of the total range. For example, if you had a table with a primary key column of id whose minimum value was 0 and maximum value was 1000, and Sqoop was directed to use 4 tasks, Sqoop would run four processes which each execute SQL statements of the form SELECT * FROM sometable WHERE id >= lo AND id < hi, with (lo, hi) set to (0, 250), (250, 500), (500, 750), and (750, 1001) in the different tasks.

> If the actual values for the primary key are not uniformly distributed across its range, then this can result in unbalanced tasks. You should explicitly choose a different column with the `--split-by` argument. For example, `--split-by` employee_id. Sqoop cannot currently split on multi-column indices. If your table has no index column, or has a multi-column key, then you must also manually choose a splitting column.

5.3.6 Incremental-Import

Sqoop provides an incremental import mode which can be used to retrieve only rows newer than some previously-imported set of rows.

The following arguments control incremental imports:

Argument	Description
--check-column (col)	Specifies the column to be examined when determining which rows to import. (the column should not be of type CHAR/NCHAR/ VARCHAR/VARNCHAR/ LONGVARCHAR/ LONGNVARCHAR)
--incremental (mode)	Specifies how Sqoop determines which rows are new. Legal values for mode include append and last modified.
--last-value (value)	Specifies the maximum value of the check column from the previous import.

<u>Step 1</u>: Import any Mysql table (ex: emp) to a new target directory on HDFS and note down the last primary key column value which has been imported.

<u>Step 2</u>: Insert new records to Mysql table (ex: emp) using Sqoop eval sub-command or login through MySQL .

<u>Step 3</u>: Perform incremental import on same HDFS target directory to load only newly added records from Mysql.

Step 1:

```
$sqoop import  --connect "jdbc:mysql://localhost/lab"
 --username nh001  --password 1234  --table emp
 --target-dir   /user/cloudera/sqimport
```

```
$hadoop fs -cat /user/cloudera/sqimport/part*
```

```
OUTPUT:
1001,ram,21
1002,sita,22
1003,ravi,23
1004,teja,21
1005,meena,22
1006,mona,20
1007,sona,21
1008,harish,23
1009,james,35
1010,Jacob,30
```

Step 2:

```
$sqoop eval --connect "jdbc:mysql://localhost/lab"
--username nh001 --password 1234 --query "insert
into emp values(1011,'jack',22),(1012,'leela',25)"
```

Step 3:

```
$ sqoop import --connect "jdbc:mysql://localhost/
lab" --username nh001 --password 1234 --table emp
--target-dir /user/cloudera/sqimport --incremental
append --check-column empno --last-value 1010
```

To check whether or not tables are imported

```
$ hadoop fs -ls /user/cloudera/sqimport
```

```
OUTPUT:
-rw-r--r-- 1 cloudera cloudera   0 2019-05-19 05:52
   /user/cloudera/sqimport/_SUCCESS
-rw-r--r-- 1 cloudera cloudera  38 2019-05-19 05:51
   /user/cloudera/sqimport/part-m-00000
-rw-r--r-- 1 cloudera cloudera  27 2019-05-19 05:51
   /user/cloudera/sqimport/part-m-00001
-rw-r--r-- 1 cloudera cloudera  26 2019-05-19 05:52
   /user/cloudera/sqimport/part-m-00002
-rw-r--r-- 1 cloudera cloudera  43 2019-05-19 05:52
   /user/cloudera/sqimport/part-m-00003
```

```
-rw-r--r--   1 cloudera cloudera   13 2019-05-19 05:58
   /user/cloudera/sqimport/part-m-00004
-rw-r--r--   1 cloudera cloudera   14 2019-05-19 05:58
   /user/cloudera/sqimport/part-m-00005
```

To check the contents of newly created directory

```
$ hadoop fs -cat /user/cloudera/sqimport/
part-m-00005
```

OUTPUT:
```
1012,leela,25
```

To see the records of Mysql table on hdfs file

```
$ hadoop fs -cat /user/cloudera/sqimport/part*
```

OUTPUT:
```
1001,ram,21
1002,sita,22
1003,ravi,23
1004,teja,21
1005,meena,22
1006,mona,20
1007,sona,21
1008,harish,23
1009,james,35
1010,jacob,30
1011,jack,22
1012,leela,25
```

5.4 EXPORT FILES FROM HDFS TO MYSQL DATABASE

The export tool exports a set of files from HDFS back to an RDBMS. The target table must already exist in the database. The input files are read and parsed into a set of records according to the user-specified delimiters.

The default operation is to transform these into a set of INSERT statements that inject the records into the database

--export-dir <dir>	HDFS source path for the export
-m, --num-mappers <n>	Use *n* map tasks to export in parallel
--table <table-name>	Table to populate

Step 1: Create a file on local file system using 'gedit' editor with default delimiter as ' , ' and save it & close.

Load this file to HDFS (default or your own directory)

```
$gedit test
1111,Teja
1112,Hari
1113,Ravi
1114,Pavan
1115,Lalit
1116,Milind
```

```
$ hadoop fs -put /home/cloudera/test /user/
cloudera/Practice/test
```

Step 2: login to MySQL and create an empty table with appropriate data type and primary key.

```
$mysql -u nh001 -p
Password:1234

mysql>use lab;
mysql>create table stud(sno int primary key,name
    varchar(10));
```

Step 3: Perform Sqoop export command to load the hdfs file to mysql table.

```
$ sqoop export --connect "jdbc:mysql://localhost/
lab" --username nh001 --password 1234 --table stud
--export-dir /user/cloudera/Practice/test
```

```
mysql> select * from stud;
+------+--------+
| sno  | name   |
+------+--------+
|  111 | Teja   |
|  112 | Mayank |
|  115 | Lalit  |
| 1111 | Teja   |
| 1112 | Hari   |
| 1113 | Ravi   |
| 1114 | Pavan  |
| 1115 | Lalit  |
| 1116 | Milind |
+------+--------+
```

5.4.1 Export With Update Key

By default, `sqoop-export` appends new rows to a table; each input record is transformed into an INSERT statement that adds a row to the target database table.

If you specify the `--update-key` argument, Sqoop will instead modify an existing dataset in the database. Each input record is treated as an UPDATE statement that modifies an existing row. The row to be modified is determined by the column name(s) specified with `--update-key`. For example, consider the following table definition which was created and loaded by Sqoop Export insert mode command:

```
mysql> create table stud(sno int primary key,name
varchar(10));
```

Also, consider a dataset in HDFS containing records like these:

```
$gedit modify
1111,Tejavati
1112,Harinath
```

Run the following command for update mode export action:

```
$ sqoop export --connect "jdbc:mysql://localhost/lab"
--username nh001 --password 1234 --table stud
--update-key sno  --export-dir /user/cloudera/
Practice/modify
```

```
OUTPUT:
mysql> select * from stud;
+------+----------+
| sno  | name     |
+------+----------+
| 1111 | Tejavati |
| 1112 | Harinath |
| 1113 | Ravi     |
| 1114 | Pavan    |
| 1115 | Lalit    |
| 1116 | Milind   |
+------+----------+
```

Running the above command will run an export job that executes SQL statements based on the data like so:

```
UPDATE stud SET name='Tejavati' WHERE sno=1111;
UPDATE stud SET name='Harinath' WHERE sno=1112;
```

The argument --update-key can also be given a comma separated list of column names. In which case, Sqoop will match all keys from this list before updating any existing record.

5.4.2 Export Using Update Mode with AllowInsert Argument

Depending on the target database, you may also specify the --update-mode argument with allowinsert mode if you want to update rows if they exist in the database already or insert rows if they do not exist yet.

Step 1: Use the same above mentioned "stud" MySQL table.

```
OUTPUT(Existing Table):
mysql> select * from stud;
+------+----------+
| sno  | name     |
+------+----------+
| 1111 | Tejavati |
| 1112 | Harinath |
| 1113 | Ravi     |
| 1114 | Pavan    |
| 1115 | Lalit    |
| 1116 | Milind   |
+------+----------+
```

Step 2: Create a file and load it to HDFS with few data to update and few new rows to insert.

```
$gedit modify2
1113,Ravi M
1115,Om Lalit
1117,Harshini
1118,Mayank
1119,Varsha
```

```
$hadoop fs -put /home/cloudera/modify2 /user/
cloudera/Practice
```

Step 3: Perform export by allowing insert in update mode

```
$sqoop export --connect "jdbc:mysql://localhost/
lab" --username nh001 --password 1234 --table
stud --update-key sno --update-mode allowinsert
--export-dir /user/cloudera/Practice/modify2
```

```
OUTPUT:
mysql> select * from stud;
+------+----------+
| sno  | name     |
+------+----------+
| 1111 | Tejavati |
| 1112 | Harinath |
| 1113 | Ravi M   |
| 1114 | Pavan    |
| 1115 | Om Lalit |
| 1116 | Milind   |
| 1117 | Harshini |
| 1118 | Mayank   |
| 1119 | Varsha   |
+------+----------+
```

5.5 SPECIFYING THE DELIMITERS TO USE IN A TEXT-MODE IMPORT/EXPORT

The default delimiters are a comma (,) for fields, a newline (\n) for records, no quote character, and no escape character. Note that this can lead to ambiguous records if you import database records containing commas or newlines in the field data.

Argument	Description
`--fields-terminated-by <char>`	Sets the field separator character
`--lines-terminated-by <char>`	Sets the end-of-line character

Delimiters may be specified as:

- a character (--fields-terminated-by X)

- an escape character (--fields-terminated-by \t). Supported escape characters are:

  ○ \b (backspace)

- ○ \n (newline)

- ○ \r (carriage return)

- ○ \t (tab)

- ○ \" (double-quote)

- ○ \' (single-quote)

- ○ \\ (backslash)

5.5.1 For Single Table Import:

Import with new delimiter

```
$sqoop import --connect "jdbc:mysql://localhost/
lab" --username nh001 --password 1234 --table emp
--fields-terminated-by '/'    --lines-terminated-by
'*' --target-dir /user/cloudera/delim
```

To Verify the newly created directory

$ hadoop fs -ls /user/cloudera/delim

```
OUTPUT:
-rw-r--r--  1 cloudera cloudera    0 2019-05-18 03:13
   /user/cloudera/delim/_SUCCESS
-rw-r--r--  1 cloudera cloudera   38 2019-05-18 03:12
   /user/cloudera/delim/part-m-00000
-rw-r--r--  1 cloudera cloudera   27 2019-05-18 03:12
   /user/cloudera/delim/part-m-00001
-rw-r--r--  1 cloudera cloudera   26 2019-05-18 03:13
   /user/cloudera/delim/part-m-00002
-rw-r--r--  1 cloudera cloudera   43 2019-05-18 03:13
   /user/cloudera/delim/part-m-00003
```

To display the content of imported file on HDFS with new delimiters

```
$ hadoop fs -cat /user/cloudera/delim/p*
```

```
OUTPUT:
1001/ram/21*1002/sita/22*1003/ravi/23*1004/
teja/21*1005/meena/22*1006/mona/20*1007/
sona/21*1008/harish/23*1009/james/35*1010/
jacob/30*
```

5.5.2 For Import-all-tables:

Import of all tables in the database with new delimiter

```
$ sqoop import-all-tables --connect "jdbc:mysql://
localhost/lab" --username nh001 --password 1234
--warehouse-dir /user/cloudera/all --fields-
terminated-by '\t' --lines-terminated-by '$'
```

> **NOTE!!!** If import has to be done on default directory then don't use `--warehouse-dir` argument in the above sqoop command.

To Verify the newly created directory

```
$hadoop fs -ls  /user/cloudera/dept
```

```
OUTPUT:
-rw-r--r--   1 cloudera cloudera    0 2019-05-18 03:37
   /user/cloudera/dept/_SUCCESS
-rw-r--r--   1 cloudera cloudera   14 2019-05-18 03:36
   /user/cloudera/dept/part-m-00000
-rw-r--r--   1 cloudera cloudera   13 2019-05-18 03:36
   /user/cloudera/dept/part-m-00001
-rw-r--r--   1 cloudera cloudera   13 2019-05-18 03:37
   /user/cloudera/dept/part-m-00002
-rw-r--r--   1 cloudera cloudera   23 2019-05-18 03:37
   /user/cloudera/dept/part-m-00003
```

To display the content of imported files on HDFS with new delimiters

```
$ hadoop fs -cat /user/cloudera/dept/p*
```

```
OUTPUT:
10 cse$20   ise$30      me$40 mba$50        mca$60
   au$70 civil$80       ece$90      eee$
```

```
$ hadoop fs -cat /user/cloudera/emp/p*
```

```
OUTPUT:
1001   ram   21$1002     sita  22$1003      ravi   23$1004
teja   21$1005   meena 22$1006   mona   20$1007
sona   21$1008   harish 23$1009   james   35$1010
jacob 30$1011   jack   22$1012   leela  25$
```

5.5.3 For Export Command:

To export files from HDFS to MySQL that has been delimited using any other single character other than default comma ','.

```
$gedit modify
101:Leela:22
102:Chaitra:25
103:Maya:26
104:Veena:24
105:Varsha:24
106:Saniya:29
```

```
$hadoop fs -put /home/cloudera/staff /user/cloudera
```

```
$ sqoop export --connect "jdbc:mysql://localhost/
lab" --username nh001 --password 1234 --table
staff  --export-dir /user/cloudera/Practice/staff
--input-fields-terminated-by ':' --input-lines-
terminated-by '\n'
```

```
OUTPUT:
mysql> select * from staff;
+-----+---------+------+
| sid | sname   | age  |
+-----+---------+------+
| 101 | Leela   |  22  |
| 102 | Chaitra |  25  |
| 103 | Maya    |  26  |
| 104 | Veena   |  24  |
| 105 | Varsha  |  24  |
| 106 | Saniya  |  29  |
+-----+---------+------+
```

5.6 SQOOP JOBS

The job tool allows you to create and work with saved jobs. Saved jobs remember the parameters used to specify a job, so they can be re-executed by invoking the job by its handle.

Creating saved jobs is done with the --create action. This operation requires

a --   followed by a space and then followed by tool name and its arguments. The tool and its arguments will form the basis of the saved job. Consider:

```
$ sqoop job --create myjob -- import --connect
"jdbc:mysql://localhost/lab" --username nh001
--password 1234 –table emp --target-dir /user/
cloudera/jobimport
```

This creates a job named myjob which can be executed later. The job is not run. This job is now available in the list of saved jobs:

```
$ sqoop job --list
Available jobs:
myjob
```

We can inspect the configuration of a job with the show action:

```
$ sqoop job --show myjob

Enter password: 1234
Job: myjob
Tool: import
Options:
----------------------------
verbose = false
hcatalog.drop.and.create.table = false
db.connect.string = jdbc:mysql://localhost/lab
codegen.output.delimiters.escape = 0
codegen.output.delimiters.enclose.required = false
codegen.input.delimiters.field = 0
split.limit = null
hbase.create.table = false
mainframe.input.dataset.type = p
db.require.password = true
hdfs.append.dir = false
db.table = emp
codegen.input.delimiters.escape = 0
accumulo.create.table = false
import.fetch.size = null
codegen.input.delimiters.enclose.required = false
db.username = nh001
reset.onemapper = false
codegen.output.delimiters.record = 10
import.max.inline.lob.size = 16777216
sqoop.throwOnError = false
hbase.bulk.load.enabled = false
hcatalog.create.table = false
db.clear.staging.table = false
codegen.input.delimiters.record = 0
enable.compression = false
hive.overwrite.table = false
hive.import = false
codegen.input.delimiters.enclose = 0
accumulo.batch.size = 10240000
hive.drop.delims = false
```

```
customtool.options.jsonmap = {}
codegen.output.delimiters.enclose = 0
hdfs.delete-target.dir = false
codegen.output.dir = .
codegen.auto.compile.dir = true
relaxed.isolation = false
mapreduce.num.mappers = 4
accumulo.max.latency = 5000
import.direct.split.size = 0
sqlconnection.metadata.transaction.isolation.
   level = 2
codegen.output.delimiters.field = 44
export.new.update = UpdateOnly
incremental.mode = None
hdfs.file.format = TextFile
sqoop.oracle.escaping.disabled = true
codegen.compile.dir = /tmp/sqoop-cloudera/compile/
   6a1869a7aaccce463b57d42fcc82159f
direct.import = false
temporary.dirRoot = _sqoop
hdfs.target.dir = /user/cloudera/jobimport
hive.fail.table.exists = false
db.batch = false
```

And if we are satisfied with it, we can run the job with `exec`:

```
[cloudera@localhost ~]$ sqoop job --exec myjob
Enter password:1234
18/02/07 20:50:24 INFO mapreduce.ImportJobBase:
   Retrieved 12 records.
```

To verify the content of newly created directory

```
$ hadoop fs -ls /user/cloudera/jobimport
```

```
OUTPUT:
-rw-r--r--  1 cloudera cloudera   0 2019-05-18 23:53
   /user/cloudera/jobimport/_SUCCESS
-rw-r--r--  1 cloudera cloudera  38 2019-05-18 23:53
   /user/cloudera/jobimport/part-m-00000
```

```
-rw-r--r--  1 cloudera cloudera  27 2019-05-18 23:53
    /user/cloudera/jobimport/part-m-00001
-rw-r--r--  1 cloudera cloudera  26 2019-05-18 23:53
    /user/cloudera/jobimport/part-m-00002
-rw-r--r--  1 cloudera cloudera  43 2019-05-18 23:53
    /user/cloudera/jobimport/part-m-00003
```

To see the records of Mysql table on hdfs file

```
$ hadoop fs -cat /user/cloudera/jobimport/p*
```

```
OUTPUT:
1001,ram,21
1002,sita,22
1003,ravi,23
1004,teja,21
1005,meena,22
1006,mona,20
1007,sona,21
1008,harish,23
1009,james,35
1010,jacob,30
```

The exec action allows you to override arguments of the saved job by supplying them after a --. For example, if the database were changed to require a username, we could specify the username and password with:

```
$ sqoop job --exec myjob -- --username someuser -P
Enter password:
...
```

Chapter 6
Pig Latin Commands

6.1 INTRODUCTION

Apache Pig is a high-level extensible language designed to reduce the complexities of coding Map-Reduce applications. It is used to load the data, apply the required filters and dump the data in the required format.

It is similar to SQL query language but applied on a larger dataset and with additional features. The language used in Pig is called **PigLatin**. Pig Latin is the language used to write Pig programs. Pig converts all the operations into Map and Reduce tasks which can be efficiently processed on Hadoop. Pig can handle any type of data, i.e., structured, semi-structured or unstructured and stores the corresponding results into Hadoop Data File System. Every task which can be achieved using PIG can also be achieved using java used in MapReduce.

Features of Apache Pig

1. **Ease of Programming:** Writing complex java programs for map reduce is quite tough for non-programmers. Pig makes this process easy. In the Pig, the queries are converted to MapReduce internally.

2. **Optimization Opportunities:** It is how tasks are encoded permits the system to optimize their execution automatically, allowing the user to focus on semantics rather than efficiency.

3. **Extensibility:** A user-defined function is written in which the user can write their logic to execute over the data set.

4. **Flexible:** It can easily handle structured as well as unstructured data.

5. **In-built Operators:** It contains various type of operators such as sort, filter and joins.

Advantages of Apache Pig

1. **Less Code:** The Pig consumes less line of code to perform any operation.

2. **Reusability:** The Pig code is flexible enough to reuse again.

3. **Nested Data Types:** The Pig provides a useful concept of nested data types like tuple, bag, and map.

Pig Execution Modes:

1. **Local Mode:** In this mode, Pig runs in a single JVM (Java Virtual Machine) and makes use of local file system. This mode is suitable only for analysis of small data sets using Pig,. Here, files are installed and run using localhost. The input and output data stored in the local file system.

   The command for local mode grunt shell:

   ```
   $ pig-x local
   ```

2. **Map Reduce Mode:** In this mode, queries written in Pig Latin are translated into MapReduce jobs and are run on a Hadoop cluster (cluster may be pseudo or fully distributed). MapReduce mode with fully distributed cluster is useful of running Pig on large data sets. Here, the input and output data are present on HDFS.

   The command for Map reduce mode:

   ```
   $ pig
   Or,
   $ pig -x mapreduce
   ```

Ways to Execute Pig Program

These are the following ways of executing a Pig program on local and MapReduce mode:

1. **Interactive Mode:** In this mode, the Pig is executed in the Grunt shell. To invoke Grunt shell, run the pig command. Once the Grunt mode executes, we can provide Pig Latin statements and command interactively at the command line.

2. **Batch Mode:** In this mode, we can run a script file having a '.pig' extension. These files contain Pig Latin commands.

3. **Embedded Mode:** In this mode, we can define our own functions. These functions can be called as UDF (User Defined Functions). Here, we use programming languages like Java and Python.

Apache Pig – Architecture

As shown in the figure below, there are various components in the Apache Pig framework.

Parser: Initially the Pig Scripts are handled by the Parser. It checks the syntax of the script, does type checking, and other miscellaneous checks. The output of the parser will be a DAG (directed acyclic graph), which represents the Pig Latin statements and logical operators.

In the DAG, the logical operators of the script are represented as the nodes and the data flows are represented as edges.

Optimizer: The logical plan (DAG) is passed to the logical optimizer, which carries out the logical optimizations such as projection and pushdown.

Compiler: The compiler compiles the optimized logical plan into a series of MapReduce jobs.

Execution Engine: Finally the MapReduce jobs are submitted to Hadoop in a sorted order. Finally, these MapReduce jobs are executed on Hadoop producing the desired results.

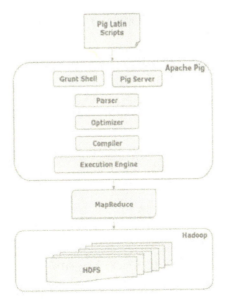

6.2 PIG LATIN BASICS

Pig Latin Data Model

Atom: Any single value in Pig Latin, irrespective of their data type is known as an **Atom.**

- A piece of data or a simple atomic value is known as a **field.**
- **Example** – 'Jay' or '35'

Tuple: A record that is formed by an ordered set of fields is known as a tuple, the fields can be of any type.

- A tuple is similar to a row in a table of RDBMS.
- **Example** –   (Jay, 35)

Bag: A bag is an unordered set of tuples.

- In other words, a collection of tuples is known as a bag.
- Each tuple can have any number of fields (flexible schema).
- A bag is represented by '{ }'. It is similar to a table in RDBMS.
- **Example** –   { (Jay, 35), (Mohan, 45)}

Map: A map (or data map) is a set of key-value pairs.

- The **key** needs to be of type chararray and should be unique.
- The **value** might be of any type. It is represented by '[ ]'
- **Example** – [name#Jay, age#35]

Relation: A bag of tuples is what we call Relation. In Pig Latin, the relations are unordered. Also, there is no guarantee that tuples are processed in any particular order.

Case Sensitivity

The names (aliases) of relations and fields are case sensitive. The names of Pig Latin functions are case sensitive. The names of parameters and all other Pig Latin keywords are case insensitive.

In the example below, note the following:

- The names (aliases) of relations A, B, and C are case sensitive.
- The names (aliases) of fields f1, f2, and f3 are case sensitive.

- Function names PigStorage and COUNT are case sensitive.

- Keywords LOAD, STORE, USING, AS, GROUP, BY, FOREACH, GENERATE, and DUMP are case insensitive. They can also be written as load, using, as, group, by, etc.

- In the FOREACH statement, the field in relation B is referred to by positional notation ($0).

```
grunt> A = LOAD 'data' USING PigStorage() AS
   (f1:int, f2:int, f3:int);
grunt> B = GROUP A BY f1;
grunt> C = FOREACH B GENERATE COUNT ($0);
grunt> DUMP C;
```

Identifiers

Identifiers include the names of relations (aliases), fields, variables, and so on. In Pig, identifiers start with a letter and can be followed by any number of letters, digits, or underscores.

Valid Identifiers:

```
A
A123
abc_123_BeX_
```

Invalid Identifiers:

```
_A123
abc_$
A!B
```

Pig Latin – Data types

S.NO	Data Type	Description & Example
1	int	Represents a signed 32-bit integer. **Example:** 8
2	long	Represents a signed 64-bit integer. **Example:** 5L
3	float	Represents a signed 32-bit floating point. **Example:** 5.5F

S.NO	Data Type	Description & Example
4	double	Represents a 64-bit floating point. **Example:** 10.5
5	chararray	Represents a character array (string) in Unicode UTF-8 format. **Example:** 'tutorials point'
6	Bytearray	Represents a Byte array (blob).
7	Boolean	Represents a Boolean value. **Example:** true/ false.
8	Datetime	Represents a date-time. **Example:** 1970-01-01T00:00:00.000+00:00
9	Biginteger	Represents a Java BigInteger. **Example:** 60708090709
10	Bigdecimal	Represents a Java BigDecimal **Example:** 185.98376256272893883
Complex Types		
11	Tuple	A tuple is an ordered set of fields. **Example:** (Jay, 35)
12	Bag	A bag is a collection of tuples. **Example:** {(Jay,35), (Mohan,45)}
13	Map	A Map is a set of key-value pairs. **Example:** ['name'#'Jay', 'age'#35]

Null Values

Values for all the above data types can be NULL. Apache Pig treats null values in a similar way as SQL does. A null can be an unknown value or a non-existent value.

6.3 RUN PIG IN INTERACTIVE MODE

MAPREDUCE MODE

Step 1: Preparing Hadoop hdfs

Verify Hadoop Daemons by typing

```
$sudo jps
```

Step 2: Create a your own directory in HDFS (optional)

```
$hadoop fs -mkdir /user/cloudera/Practice
```

Step 3: Load the data on hdfs

Create a file on local file system with delimiter ',' and copy it on to HDFS your directory

```
$gedit doctor.csv
Milan,1001,5,apollo,500
Jay,1002,10,Apollo,500
Lalit,1003,20,manipal,500
Mohit,1004,15,Columbia,600
Chauhan,1005,30,narayana,550
Suraj,1006,25,manipal,650
Jay,102,10,apollo,50
```

- **Load it on to hdfs**

  ```
  $hadoop fs -put /home/cloudera/doctor.csv
  /user/cloudera/Practice
  ```

- **Verify the file on hdfs (your folder)**

  ```
  $hadoop fs -cat /user/cloudera/Practice/
  doctor.csv
  ```

  (OR)

- **Verify the output through browser**

  ```
  Click on "Hadoop→HDFS Namenode→Utilities→
  Browse the file system→\→user→cloudera→
  Practice→doctor.csv
  ```

Step 4: Run Apache Pig in mapreduce mode

```
$pig
(or)
$pig -x mapreduce

grunt>
```

LOCAL MODE

Step 1: Preparing Hadoop hdfs

Verify Hadoop Daemons by typing

```
$sudo jps
```

Step 2: Load the data on hdfs

Create a file on local file system with delimiter ' , ' and copy it on to HDFS your directory

```
$gedit doctor.csv
Milan,1001,5,apollo,500
Jay,1002,10,apollo,500
Lalit,1003,20,manipal,500
Mohit,1004,15,Columbia,600
Chauhan,1005,30,narayana,550
Suraj,1006,25,manipal,650
Jay,1002,10,apollo,500
```

Step 3: Run Apache Pig in mapreduce mode

```
$pig -x local
grunt>
```

fs Command

Using the **fs** command, we can invoke any FsShell commands from the Grunt shell.

Syntax:

```
grunt> fs<File System command parameters>
```

Example:

We can invoke the ls command of HDFS from the Grunt shell using fs command. In the following example, it lists the files in the HDFS '/user/cloudera 'directory.

```
grunt> fs -ls /user/cloudera
```

6.4 LOAD & STORE

> **NOTE !!!**
> In Pig Latin Statements, there must be space before and after the equal '=' symbol.

6.4.1 Mapreduce Mode

Load the file stored on hdfs to pigstorage for analysis using 'LOAD' operator

```
Syntax:
Relation_name = LOAD 'Input file path' USING
    function as schema;
```

The load statement consists of two parts divided by the "=" operator. Where,

- **relation_name** – the relation in which we want to store the data.

- **Input file path** – the HDFS directory where the file is stored. (In MapReduce mode)

- **function** – choose a function from the set of load functions provided by Apache Pig (**BinStorage, JsonLoader, PigStorage, TextLoader**).

- **Schema** - define the schema of the data. It is optional. We can define the required schema as follows:

```
(column1 : data type, column2 : data type, column3
    : data type);
```

Note!!! If we load the data without specifying the schema, the columns will be addressed as $01, $02, etc....

Example:

```
grunt> doc = LOAD '/user/cloudera/Practice/
    doctor.csv' USING PigStorage(',') as
(name:chararray,id:int,exp:int,hosp:chararray,
    fees:int);
```

To display the output of Pigstorage to the console, use diagnostic operator 'dump.'

```
grunt> Dump doc;
```

To store the output of Pigstorage after analysis on to the HDFS.

Store the loaded data in the file system using the **store** operator.

```
Syntax:
STORE Relation_name INTO 'required_directory_path
  '[USING function];

Example:
grunt> STORE doc INTO '/user/cloudera/Practice/
  out' USING PigStorage(',');
```

Here,

doctor   : is relation name on pig

*/user/cloudera/Practice/***out** : is the path where you want to store the
relation from pig storage after analysis
to HDFS (in mapreduce mode) for
permanent store. Also new directory
name (say, **out**) has to be mentioned as
your output will be in part file which will
be inside this new directory.

To verify the content of newly created directory

```
$ hadoop fs -ls /user/cloudera/Practice/out
```

To verify the stored file on hdfs

```
$ hadoop fs -cat /user/cloudera/Practice/out/
  part-m-00000
```
                        (OR)
```
$ hadoop fs -cat /user/cloudera/Practice/out/p*
```

6.4.2 Local Mode

Load the file stored on local filesystem to pigstorage for analysis using
'LOAD' operator

```
Syntax:
Relation_name = LOAD 'Input file path' USING
  function as schema;
```

```
Example:
grunt> doc = LOAD '/home/cloudera/doctor.csv'
   USING PigStorage(',') as
(name:chararray,id:int,exp:int,hosp:chararray,
   fees:int);
```

The load statement consists of two parts divided by the "=" operator. Here also schema is optional.

To display the output of Pigstorage to the console, use diagnostic operator 'dump.'

```
grunt> Dump doc;
```

To store the output of Pigstorage after analysis on to the Local Filesystem (say, Desktop).

Store the loaded data in the file system using the **store** operator.

```
Syntax:
STORE Relation_name INTO 'required_directory_path
   '[USING function];
```

```
Example:
grunt> STORE doctor INTO '/home/cloudera/Desktop/
   out' USING PigStorage(',');
```

Here,

doctor   : is relation name on pig

/home/cloudera/Desktop/out   : is the path where you want to store the relation from pig after analysis to local file system's desktop (in local mode) for permanent store. Also new directory name (say, **out**) has to be mentioned as your output will be in part file which will be inside this new directory.

To verify the content of newly created directory

```
$ cd /home/cloudera/Desktop/out
$ ls
$ cat part-m-00000
(OR)
```

Directly double click the part file created on cloudera desktop.

6.5 UTILITY COMMAND AND DIAGNOSTIC OPERATORS

6.5.1 Utility Commands

1. **clear** Command: The **clear** command is used to clear the screen of the Grunt shell.

   ```
   grunt> clear
   ```

2. **help** Command: The **help** command gives you a list of Pig commands or Pig properties.

   ```
   grunt> help
   ```

3. **history** Command: This command displays a list of statements executed / used so far since the Grunt sell is invoked.

   ```
   grunt> history
   ```

4. **quit** Command: You can quit from the Grunt shell using this command.

   ```
   grunt> quit
   ```

Diagnostic Operators

Pig Latin provides four different types of diagnostic operators –

- Dump operator
- Describe operator
- Explanation operator
- Illustration operator

6.5.2 Diagnostic Operators

Dump Operator: It is used to run the Pig Latin statements and display the results on the screen. It is generally used for debugging Purpose.

```
Syntax:
grunt>Dump Relation_Name

Example:
grunt> doc = LOAD '/user/cloudera/
Practice/doctor.csv' USING PigStorage(',') as
    (name:chararray,id:int,exp:int,hosp:chararray,
    fees:int);

grunt> dump doc;
(Milan,1001,5,apollo,500)
(Jay,1002,10,apollo,500)
(lalit,1003,20,manipal,500)
(Mohit,1004,15,Columbia,600)
(Chauhan,1005,30,narayana,550)
(Suraj,1006,25,manipal,650)
(Jay,1002,10,apollo,500)
```

Describe Operator: It is used to view the schema of a relation.

```
Syntax:
grunt> Describe Relation_name

grunt> describe doc;
doc: {name: chararray,id: int,exp: int,hosp:
    chararray,fees: int}
```

Explain Operator: It is used to display the logical, physical, and MapReduce execution plans of a relation.

```
Syntax:
grunt> explain Relation_name;
grunt> explain doc;
```

Illustrate Operator: It gives you the step-by-step execution of a sequence of statements.

```
Syntax:
grunt> illustrate Relation_name;

grunt> illustrate doc;
-----------------------------------------------------------------
|doc| name:chararray| id:int| exp:int| hosp:chararray| fees:int|
-----------------------------------------------------------------
|    |Jay            | 1002  | 10     | Apollo        | 500     |
-----------------------------------------------------------------

grunt> illustrate doc;
-----------------------------------------------------------------
| doc| name:chararray| id:int| exp:int| hosp:chararray| fees:int|
-----------------------------------------------------------------
|    | Suraj         | 1006  | 25     | manipal       | 650     |
-----------------------------------------------------------------
```

NOTE!!!!
Question: Can we load the file to pig without schema?
Ans: Yes

```
grunt> doc = LOAD '/user/cloudera/Practice/doctor.
   csv' USING PigStorage(',');

grunt> describe doc;
Schema for doc unknown.

grunt> dump doc;
(Milan,1001,5,apollo,500)
(Jay,1002,10,apollo,500)
(lalit,1003,20,manipal,500)
(Mohit,1004,15,Columbia,600)
(Chauhan,1005,30,narayana,550)
(Suraj,1006,25,manipal,650)
(Jay,1002,10,apollo,500)
```

In this case, we need to use positional notation like $0, $1 etc. to denote the fields in the relation.

6.6 APACHE-PIG BASIC OPERATORS

6.6.1 Arthematic Operators

The following table describes the arithmetic operators of Pig Latin. Suppose a = 10 and b = 20.

Operator	Description	Example
+	**Addition** – Adds values on either side of the operator	a + b will give 30
–	**Subtraction** – Subtracts right hand operand from left hand operand	a – b will give –10
*	**Multiplication** – Multiplies values on either side of the operator	a * b will give 200
/	**Division** – Divides left hand operand by right hand operand	b / a will give 2
%	**Modulus** – Divides left hand operand by right hand operand and returns remainder	b % a will give 0
bincond	? : :	(condition? value_if_true: value_if_false) The bincond should be enclosed in parenthesis. The schemas for the two conditional outputs of the bincond should match. Use expressions only (relational operators are not allowed).

6.6.2 Comparison Operators

The following table describes the comparison operators of Pig Latin.

Operator	Description	Example
==	**Equal** – Checks if the values of two operands are equal or not; if yes, then the condition becomes true.	(a = b) is not true

Operator	Description	Example
!=	**Not Equal** – Checks if the values of two operands are equal or not. If the values are not equal, then condition becomes true.	(a != b) is true.
>	**Greater than** – Checks if the value of the left operand is greater than the value of the right operand. If yes, then the condition becomes true.	(a > b) is not true.
<	**Less than** – Checks if the value of the left operand is less than the value of the right operand. If yes, then the condition becomes true.	(a < b) is true.
>=	**Greater than or equal to** – Checks if the value of the left operand is greater than or equal to the value of the right operand. If yes, then the condition becomes true.	(a >= b) is not true.
<=	**Less than or equal to** – Checks if the value of the left operand is less than or equal to the value of the right operand. If yes, then the condition becomes true.	(a <= b) is true.
matches	**Pattern matching** – Checks whether the string in the left-hand side matches with the constant in the right-hand side.	f1 matches '.*tutorial.*'

6.6.3 Filtering Operators

Three operators are used for filtering:

- FILTER Operator
- FOREACH Operator
- Distinct Operator

Filter: It is used to select the required tuples from a relation based on a condition.

```
Syntax:
grunt> Relation2_name = FILTER Relation1_name BY
   (condition);

grunt> describe doc;
doc: {name: chararray,id: int,exp: int,hosp:
   chararray,fees: int}

grunt> a = filter doc by exp>10;        (OR)
grunt> a = filter doc by $2>10;
grunt>dump a;
(lalit,1003,20,manipal,500)
(Mohit,1004,15,columbia,600)
(Chauhan,1005,30,narayana,550)
(Suraj,1006,25,manipal,650)
```

Distinct: It is used to remove redundant (duplicate) tuples from a relation.

```
Syntax:
grunt> Relation_name2 = DISTINCT Relatin_name1;

grunt> dump doc;
(Milan,1001,5,apollo,500)
(Jay,1002,10,apollo,500)
(lalit,1003,20,manipal,500)
(Mohit,1004,15,columbia,600)
(Chauhan,1005,30,narayana,550)
(Suraj,1006,25,manipal,650)
(Jay,1002,10,apollo,500)
grunt> a = distinct doc;
grunt> dump a;
(Jay,1002,10,apollo,500)
(Milan,1001,5,apollo,500)
(Mohit,1004,15,columbia,600)
(Suraj,1006,25,manipal,650)
(lalit,1003,20,manipal,500)
(Chauhan,1005,30,narayana,550)
```

Here, (Jay,1002,10,apollo,500) is repeated in dataset to show the use of distinct keyword.

For the remaining below exercises,

- remove the repeated line (Jay,1002,10,apollo,500) from the dataset

- save the file and load it to HDFS as doc.csv.

- Run the Pig in MapReduce mode and perform load as shown below.

Foreach: It is used to generate specified data transformations based on the column data.

```
Syntax:
grunt> Relation_name2 = FOREACH Relatin_name1
    GENERATE (required data);
```

```
Example 1:

Projection: The asterisk (*) is used to project all fields from relation
"doc" to relation "doc1". Relation doc and doc1 are identical.
grunt> doc = LOAD '/user/cloudera/
Practice/doc.csv' USING PigStorage(',') as
    (name:chararray,id:int,exp:int,hosp:chararray,
    fees:int);

grunt> dump doc;
(Milan,1001,5,apollo,500)
(Jay,1002,10,Apollo,500)
(lalit,1003,20,manipal,500)
(Mohit,1004,15,Columbia,600)
(Chauhan,1005,30,narayana,550)
(Suraj,1006,25,manipal,650)

grunt> doc1 = foreach doc generate *;
grunt> dump doc1;
(Jay,1002,10,apollo,500)
(Milan,1001,5,apollo,500)
(Mohit,1004,15,columbia,600)
(Suraj,1006,25,manipal,650)
(lalit,1003,20,manipal,500)
(Chauhan,1005,30,narayana,550)
```

```
Example 2:
grunt> a = foreach doc generate name,hosp;     (OR)
grunt> a = foreach doc generate $0,$3;
grunt> dump a;
(Milan,apollo)
(Jay,apollo)
(lalit,manipal)
(Mohit,columbia)
(Chauhan,narayana)
(Suraj,manipal)
```

6.6.4 Analyze the Doctor Dataset Using Various Basic Operators

Q) List different fees taken by various doctors.

```
grunt> a = foreach doc generate fees;
grunt> ans = distinct a;
grunt> dump ans;
```

```
OUTPUT:
(500)
(550)
(650)
(600)
```

Q) Display doctor name, hospital name, fees on to the console.

```
grunt> a = foreach doc generate name,hosp,fees;
grunt> dump a;
```

```
OUTPUT:
(Milan,apollo,500)
(Jay,apollo,500)
(lalit,manipal,500)
(Mohit,columbia,600)
(Chauhan,narayana,550)
(Suraj,manipal,650)
```

Q) Display the details of doctor who works in apollo hospital.

```
grunt> a = filter doc by hosp=='apollo';
grunt> dump a;
```

> **OUTPUT:**
> *(Milan,1001,5,apollo,500)*
> *(Jay,1002,10,apollo,500)*

Q) Display only doctor name, doctor id who works in manipal hospital.

```
grunt> a = filter doc by hosp=='manipal';
grunt> ans = foreach a generate name,id;
grunt> dump ans;
```

> **OUTPUT:**
> *(lalit,1003)*
> *(Suraj,1006)*

Queries on Arthematic, comparision and Boolean operator

Q) Display doctor name, fees, fees%10

```
grunt> a = foreach doc generate name, fees,
    fees%100;
grunt> dump a;
```

> **OUTPUT:**
> *(Milan,500,0)*
> *(Jay,500,0)*
> *(lalit,500,0)*
> *(Mohit,600,0)*
> *(Chauhan,550,50)*
> *(Suraj,650,50)*

Q) Display doctor name, hospital name, fees, fees after 10 percentage hike.

```
grunt> a = foreach doc generate name,hosp,fees,
    fees*1.1;
grunt> dump a;
```

```
OUTPUT:
(Milan,apollo,500,550.0)
(Jay,apollo,500,550.0)
(lalit,manipal,500,550.0)
(Mohit,columbia,600,660)
(Chauhan,narayana,550,605.0)
(Suraj,manipal,650,715.0000000000001)
```

Q) Display doctor name, current fees, current fees-100 as 'new fees';

```
grunt> a = foreach doc generate name, fees,
    fees-100 as new fees;
grunt> dump a;
```

```
OUTPUT:
(Milan,500,400)
(Jay,500,400)
(lalit,500,400)
(Mohit,600,500)
(Chauhan,550,450)
(Suraj,650,550)
```

Q) From the above output, list doctor names whose new fees is above 500.

```
grunt> ans = filter a by newfees>500;
grunt> dump ans;
```

```
OUTPUT:
(Suraj,650,550)
```

Q) Display true if experience of doctor is above 10; else display false.

```
grunt> a = foreach doc generate
    name,exp,(exp>10?'true':'false');
grunt> dump a;
```

```
OUTPUT:
(Milan,5,false)
(Jay,10,false)
(lalit,20,true)
```

```
(Mohit,15,true)
(Chauhan,30,true)
(Suraj,25,true)
```

Q) Display only hospital name, fees by taking into consideration that some concession is going on for all branches of Apollo hospital by Rs. 200. So, display new fees for Apollo hospitals and same current fees for other hospitals.

```
grunt> a = foreach doc generate
    hosp, (hosp=='apollo'?fees-200:fees);
grunt> dump a;
```

```
OUTPUT:
(apollo,300)
(apollo,300)
(manipal,500)
(columbia,600)
(narayana,550)
(manipal,650)
```

Q) Display the details of doctor whose experience is more than 20 years but not working in Manipal.

```
grunt> a = filter doc by exp>20 and hosp!='manipal';
grunt> dump a;
```

```
OUTPUT:
(Chauhan,1005,30,narayana,550)
```

(OR)

```
grunt> a = filter doc by exp>20 and not(hosp==
    'manipal');
grunt> dump a;
```

```
OUTPUT:
(Chauhan,1005,30,narayana,550)
```

Q) Display the details of doctor who is either taking fees above rs 500 or whose experience is above 20 years.

```
grunt> a = filter doc by fees>500 or exp>20;          (OR)
grunt> a = filter doc by (fees>500) or (exp>20); (OR)
grunt> a = filter doc by $4>500 or $2>20;
grunt> dump a;
```

> **OUTPUT:**
> *(Mohit,1004,15,columbia,600)*
> *(Chauhan,1005,30,narayana,550)*
> *(Suraj,1006,25,manipal,650)*

> **NOTE!!!**
> **For Pattern matching**
> *(.)   -> indicates single character*
> *(.+) -> indicates one or more characters*
> *(.*) -> indicates zero or more characters*

Q) Display the details of doctor whose name with substring 'an'

```
grunt> a = filter doc by name matches '.*an.*';
grunt> dump a;
```

> **OUTPUT:**
> *(Milan,1001,5,apollo,500)*
> *(Chauhan,1005,30,narayana,550)*

Q) Display the details of doctor whose name has 'a' substring

```
grunt> a = filter doc by name matches '.*a.*';
```

> **OUTPUT:**
> *(Milan,1001,5,apollo,500)*
> *(Jay,1002,10,apollo,500)*
> *(lalit,1003,20,manipal,500)*
> *(Chauhan,1005,30,narayana,550)*
> *(Suraj,1006,25,manipal,650)*

Q) Display the details of doctor whose name begins with 'S'

```
grunt> a = filter doc by name matches 'S.*';
```

```
OUTPUT:
(Suraj,1006,25,manipal,650)
```

Q) Display the details of doctor whose name has substring 'it'

```
grunt> a = filter doc by name matches '.*it.*';
```

```
OUTPUT:
(lalit,1003,20,manipal,500)
(Mohit,1004,15,columbia,600)
```

Q) Display the details of doctor whose hospital name has substring 'a'

```
grunt> a = filter doc by hosp matches '.*a.*';
```

```
OUTPUT:
(Milan,1001,5,apollo,500)
(Jay,1002,10,apollo,500)
(lalit,1003,20,manipal,500)
(Mohit,1004,15,columbia,600)
(Chauhan,1005,30,narayana,550)
(Suraj,1006,25,manipal,650)
```

Q) Display the details of doctor whose hospital name ends with 'a'

```
grunt> a = filter doc by hosp matches '.*a';
```

```
OUTPUT:
(Mohit,1004,15,columbia,600)
(Chauhan,1005,30,narayana,550)
```

Q) Display the details of doctor whose name has 'a' in second letter position.

```
a = filter doc by name matches '.a.*';
```

```
OUTPUT:
(Jay,1002,10,Apollo,500)
(Lalit,1003,20,manipal,500)
```

Q) Display the details of doctor whose name is a 5 letter word and ends with 't'.

```
grunt> a = filter doc by name matches '....t';
```

```
OUTPUT:
(lalit,1003,20,manipal,500)
(Mohit,1004,15,columbia,600)
```

Q) Display the details of doctor whose name is atleast a 4 letter word.

```
a = filter doc by name matches '...(.+)';          (OR)
a = filter doc by name matches '....(.*)';
```

```
OUTPUT:
(Milan,1001,5,apollo,500)
(Lalit,1003,20,manipal,500)
(Mohit,1004,15,Columbia,600)
(Chauhan,1005,30,narayana,550)
(Suraj,1006,25,manipal,650)
```

6.7 GROUPING AND JOINING OPERATOR

There are two operators for grouping the data:

- GROUP
- CO-GROUP

The Operator used for joining the data is:

- JOIN (Inner or Self Join)

6.7.1 Group Operator

The **GROUP** operator is used to group the data in the relations. It collects the data having the same key.

```
Syntax:
grunt> Group_data = GROUP Relation_name BY age;
```

Example: Display the details of doctor hospital wise.

```
grunt> gr = group doc by hosp;
grunt> dump gr;
```

OUTPUT:

```
(apollo,{(Milan,1001,5,apollo,500),
    (Jay,1002,10,apollo,500)})
(manipal,{(lalit,1003,20,manipal,500),
    (Suraj,1006,25,manipal,650)})
(columbia,{(Mohit,1004,15,columbia,600)})
(narayana,{(Chauhan,1005,30,narayana,550)})
```

Here, the resulting schema has two columns –

- One is hospital name, by which we have grouped the relation.

- The other is a bag, which contains the group of tuples (doctor details) with the respective hospital name.

```
grunt> describe gr;
```

```
gr: {group: chararray, doc:{(name: chararray,id:
    int,exp: int,hosp: chararray,fees: int)}}
```

Here, the resulting schema has two fields:

- The first field is named "group", which has the same datatype as the group key.

- The second field takes the name of the original relation and its datatype is bag

*** These two fields can be referred using positional notation also I.e. the first field "group" can be denoted by '$0' and second field "doc (inner bag as whole)" can be denoted by $1

```
grunt> illustrate gr;
```

doc	name:chararray	id:int	exp:int	hosp:chararray	fees:int
	Jay	1002	10	apollo	500
	Milan	1001	5	apollo	500

gr	group:chararray	doc:bag{:tuple(name:chararray,id:int,exp:int,hosp:chararray,fees:int)}
	apollo	{(Jay, ..., 500), (Milan, ..., 500)}

```
grunt> illustrate gr;
```

doc	name:chararray	id:int	exp:int	hosp:chararray	fees:int
	Lalit	1003	20	manipal	500
	Suraj	1006	25	manipal	650

gr	group:chararray	doc:bag{:tuple(name:chararray,id:int,exp:int,hosp:chararray,fees:int)}
	manipal	{(Lalit, ..., 500), (Suraj, ..., 650)}

> **NOTE!!!!**
>
> If one of fields in the input relation is a tuple or bag or map, then to refer the fields present inside these tuple/ bag / map, we use dereference operator dot " . "
>
> *For Example:* In the below query "gr" is the relation formed as a result of group operator and to refer the fields (name, id, exp, hosp, fees) that are present inside the inner bag "doc", we need to use dereference operator.

Q) Display the hospital name along with the doctor names who belongs to each hospital.

```
grunt> gr = group doc by hosp;
grunt> ans = foreach gr generate group,doc.name;
grunt> dump ans;
```

> **OUTPUT:**
> (apollo, { (Milan) , (Jay) })
> (manipal, { (lalit) , (Suraj) })
> (columbia, { (Mohit) })
> (narayana, { (Chauhan) })

Q) Display the doctor names and their experience hospital wise.

```
grunt> gr = group doc by hosp;
grunt> ans = foreach gr generate $0,$1.name,$1.exp;
grunt> dump ans;
```

> **OUTPUT:**
> (apollo, { (Milan) , (Jay) }, { (5) , (10) })
> (manipal, { (lalit) , (Suraj) }, { (20) , (25) })
> (columbia, { (Mohit) }, { (15) })
> (narayana, { (Chauhan) }, { (30) })

Q) Display doctor details hospital name wise and display no:of doctors in each hospital.

```
grunt> gr = group doc by hosp;
grunt> describe gr;
```

```
gr: {group: chararray,doc: {(name: chararray,id:
    int,exp: int,hosp: chararray,fees: int)}}
```

```
grunt> dump gr;
```

```
(apollo,{(Milan,1001,5,apollo,500),(Jay,1002,10,
    apollo,500)})
(manipal,{(lalit,1003,20,manipal,500),(Suraj,1006,
    25,manipal,650)})
(columbia,{(Mohit,1004,15,columbia,600)})
(narayana,{(Chauhan,1005,30,narayana,550)})
```

```
grunt> ans = foreach gr generate group,COUNT(doc);
grunt> dump ans;
```

```
OUTPUT:
(apollo,2)
(manipal,2)
(columbia,1)
(narayana,1)
```

Cast Operators And Alias

Cast operators enable you to cast or convert data from one type to another, as long as conversion is supported.

A field can be explicitly cast. Once cast, the field remains that type (it is not automatically cast back). In this example fees field is explicitly cast to float.

Example 1:
```
grunt> B = foreach doc generate (float)fees;
```

```
grunt> describe B;
B: {fees: float}
```

```
grunt> dump B;
(500.0)
(500.0)
(500.0)
(600.0)
(550.0)
(650.0)
(500.0)
```

Pig performs implicit casts also. In the below example exp is cast to int (regardless of underlying data) and fees is cast to double.

Example 2:
```
grunt> res = foreach doc generate exp+5,
    fees+1100.50;                                              (OR)
grunt> res = foreach doc generate $2+5,$4+1100.50;
```

```
grunt> describe res;
res: {int,double}

grunt> dump B;
(10,1600.5)
(15,1600.5)
(25,1600.5)
(20,1700.5)
(35,1650.5)
(30,1750.5)
(15,1600.5)
```

Example 3:

In this example a new alias name "total" is given to the field obtained on count aggregate function.

```
grunt> gr = group doc by hosp;
grunt> ans = foreach gr generate group,COUNT(doc)
    as total;
grunt> describe ans;
ans: {group: chararray,total: long}
```

Example 4:

Explicit type cast of COUNT field to chararray with alias name "total."

```
grunt> gr = group doc by hosp;
grunt> ans = foreach gr generate group, (chararray)
  COUNT(doc) as total;
grunt> describe ans;
ans: {group: chararray,total: chararray}
```

Grouping By Multiple Columns

Q) Display details of doctor hospital wise with same fees

```
grunt> a = group doc by (hosp,fees);
grunt> dump a;
```

```
OUTPUT:
((apollo,500),{(Milan,1001,5,apollo,500),
  (Jay,1002,10,apollo,500)})
((manipal,500),{(lalit,1003,20,manipal,500)})
((manipal,650),{(Suraj,1006,25,manipal,650)})
((columbia,600),{(Mohit,1004,15,columbia,600)})
((narayana,550),{(Chauhan,1005,30,narayana,550)})
```

Group All

```
grunt> a = group doc all;
grunt> dump a;
```

```
OUTPUT:
(all,{(Milan,1001,5,apollo,500),(Jay,1002,10,
  apollo,500),(lalit,1003,20,manipal,500),
  (Mohit,1004,15,columbia,600),(Chauhan,1005,
  30,narayana,550),(Suraj,1006,25,manipal,650),
  (,,,,)})
```

6.7.2 Co-Group Operator

The **COGROUP** operator works more or less in the same way as the GROUP operator. The only difference between the two operators is that the GROUP operator is normally used with one relation, while the CO-GROUP operator is used in statements involving two or more relations.

Assume two files as follows:

doctor.csv
```
Milan,1001,5,apollo,500
Jay,1002,10,apollo,500
lalit,1003,20,manipal,500
Mohit,1004,15,columbia,600
Chauhan,1005,30,narayana,550
Suraj,1006,25,manipal,650
```

emp.csv
```
7001,ameena,10,bang
7002,amit,20,chennai
7003,anand,30,bang
7004,alen,15,hyd
7005,alester,10,hyd
7006,anshul,5,chennai
```

```
grunt> doc = LOAD '/user/cloudera/Practice/
    doctor.csv' USING PigStorage(',') as
    (name:chararray,id:int,exp:int,hosp:chararray,
    fees:int);

grunt> emp = LOAD '/user/cloudera/Practice/
    emp.csv' USING PigStorage(',') as (id:int,
    name:chararray,exp:int,place:chararray);

grunt> describe doc;
```

```
doc: {name: chararray,id: int,exp: int,hosp:
    chararray,fees: int}
```

```
grunt> describe emp;
```

```
emp: {id: int,name: chararray,exp: int,place:
    chararray}
```

```
grunt> a = cogroup doc by exp,emp by exp;
grunt> describe a;
```

```
a: {group: int,doc: {(name: chararray,id:
    int,exp: int,hosp: chararray,fees: int)},
    emp: {(id: int,name: chararray,
    exp: int,place: chararray)}}
```

grunt> dump a;

```
OUTPUT:
(5,{(Milan,1001,5,apollo,500)},{(7006,anshul,
    5,chennai)})
(10,{(Jay,1002,10,apollo,500)},{(7001,ameena,
    10,bang),(7005,alester,10,hyd)})
(15,{(Mohit,1004,15,columbia,600)},{(7004,alen,
    15,hyd)})
(20,{(lalit,1003,20,manipal,500)},{(7002,amit,
    20,chennai)})
(25,{(Suraj,1006,25,manipal,650)},{})
(30,{(Chauhan,1005,30,narayana,550)},{(7003,anand,
    30,bang)})
```

The **cogroup** operator groups the tuples from each relation according to "exp" where each group depicts a particular "exp" value.

For example, if we consider the 1st tuple of the result, it is grouped by exp 5. And it contains two bags –

- the first bag holds all the tuples from the first relation (**doctor. csv** in this case) having experience of 5, and

- the second bag contains all the tuples from the second relation (**emp.csv** in this case) having experience of 5.

For co-group value "25", there is no tuple in employee dataset with experience of 25 years. So, the second bag is an empty bag.

6.7.3 Join Operator

The **JOIN** operator is used to combine records from two or more relations. While performing a join operation, we declare one (or a group of) tuple(s) from each relation, as keys. When these keys match, the two particular tuples are matched, else the records are dropped. Joins can be of the following types –

- Self-join

- Inner-join

- Outer-join – left join, right join, and full join

Self-Join

Self-join is used to join a table with itself as if the table were two relations, temporarily renaming at least one relation.

Generally, in Apache Pig, to perform self-join, we will load the same data multiple times, under different aliases (names). Therefore, let us load the contents of the file **doctor.csv** as two tables as shown below.

```
grunt> doc = LOAD '/user/cloudera/Practice/
    doctor.csv' USING PigStorage(',') as (name:
    chararray,id:int,exp:int,hosp:chararray,
    fees:int);
grunt> dump doc;
grunt> doc1 = LOAD '/user/cloudera/Practice/
    doctor.csv' USING PigStorage(',') as
    (name:chararray,id:int,exp:int,hosp:chararray,
    fees:int);
grunt> dump doc1;
```

```
grunt> a = join doc by id,doc1 by id;
grunt> dump a;
```

```
OUTPUT:
(Milan,1001,5,apollo,500,Milan,1001,5,
    apollo,500)
(Jay,1002,10,apollo,500,Jay,1002,10,apollo,500)
(lalit,1003,20,manipal,500,lalit,1003,20,
    manipal,500)
(Mohit,1004,15,columbia,600,Mohit,1004,15,
    columbia,600)
(Chauhan,1005,30,narayana,550,Chauhan,1005,30,
    narayana,550)
(Suraj,1006,25,manipal,650,Suraj,1006,25,
    manipal,650)
```

Inner Join

Inner Join is used quite frequently; it is also referred to as **equi-join**. An inner join returns rows when there is a match in both tables.

It creates a new relation by combining column values of two relations (**say A and B**) based upon the join-predicate. The query compares each row of A with each row of B to find all pairs of rows which satisfy the join-predicate. When the join-predicate is satisfied, the column values for each matched pair of rows of A and B are combined into a result row.

```
Syntax:
grunt> result = JOIN relation1 BY columnname,
    relation2 BY columnname;
```

Assume two files for joining as:

doctor.csv
```
Milan,1001,5,apollo,500
Jay,1002,10,apollo,500
lalit,1003,20,manipal,500
Mohit,1004,15,columbia,600
Chauhan,1005,30,narayana,550
Suraj,1006,25,manipal,650
```

patient.csv
```
101,harinath,5,domlur,1004
102,nagarjun,10,varthur,1005
103,chirajeevi,20,HAL,1006
104,tarun,25,HSR,1004
105,prabas,15,marthahalli,1006
106,chaitanya,30,belandur,1003
107,nani,27,krpuram,1004
```

```
grunt> doc = LOAD '/user/cloudera/Practice/
    doctor.csv' USING PigStorage(',') as
    (name:chararray,id:int,exp:int,hosp:chararray,
    fees:int);
```

```
grunt> pat = LOAD '/user/cloudera/Practice/
   patient.csv' USING PigStorage(',') as
   (pid:int,pname:chararray,age:int,place:
   chararray,docid:int);

grunt> describe doc;
doc: {name: chararray,id: int,exp: int,hosp:
   chararray,fees: int}

grunt> describe pat;
pat: {pid: int,pname: chararray,age: int,
   place: chararray, docid: int}
```

Q) Display entire details of patient and their corresponding doctor

```
grunt> a = join doc by id,pat by docid;
grunt> dump a;
```

```
OUTPUT:
(lalit,1003,20,manipal,500,106,chaitanya,30,
   belandur,1003)
(Mohit,1004,15,columbia,600,101,harinath,5,
   domlur,1004)
(Mohit,1004,15,columbia,600,104,tarun,25,
   HSR,1004)
(Mohit,1004,15,columbia,600,107,nani,27,
   krpuram,1004)
(Chauhan,1005,30,narayana,550,102,nagarjun,10,
   varthur,1005)
(Suraj,1006,25,manipal,650,103,chirajeevi,20,
   HAL,1006)
(Suraj,1006,25,manipal,650,105,prabas,15,
   marthahalli,1006)

grunt> describe a;
a: {doc::name: chararray,doc::id: int,doc::exp:
   int,doc::hosp: chararray,doc::fees: int,
   pat::pid: int,pat::pname: chararray,pat::age:
   int,pat::place: chararray,pat::docid: int}
```

Q) Display patient name, patient age along with the doctor name and hospital name where the patient has visited.

```
grunt> res = foreach a generate
pat::pname,pat::age,doc::name,doc::hosp;
grunt> dump res;
```

```
OUTPUT:
(chaitanya,30,Lalit,manipal)
(nani,27,Mohit,Columbia)
(tarun,25,Mohit,Columbia)
(harinath,5,Mohit,Columbia)
(nagarjun,10,Chauhan,narayana)
(prabas,15,Suraj,manipal)
(chirajeevi,20,Suraj,manipal)
```

> **NOTE!!!**
>
> If there is no ambiguity in the field names after joining of relations, then queries on this joined relation can be performed by using their field name only (i,e. no need of mentioning specific relation name)
>
> **For example:**
> ```
> grunt> res = foreach a generate pname,age,name,
>     hosp;
> ```

Left Outer Join

The left outer Join operation returns all rows from the left table, even if there are no matches in the right relation.

Assume two files for left & right outer joins as:

doc1.csv
```
Milan,1001,5,apollo,500
Jay,1002,10,apollo,500
Lalit,1003,20,manipal,500
Mohit,1004,15,Columbia,600
Chauhan,1005,30,narayana,550
Suraj,1006,25,manipal,650
Jayanth,1007,13,apollo,550
```

pat1.csv

```
101,harinath,5,domlur,1004
102,nagarjun,10,varthur,1005
103,chirajeevi,20,HAL,1006
104,tarun,25,HSR,1004
105,prabas,15,marthahalli,1006
106,chaitanya,30,belandur,1003
107,nani,27,krpuram,1004
108,varun,23,HSR,Null,null
109,karthik,10,varthur,null
```

Loading of above two files from HDFS to PigStorage.

```
doc1 = LOAD '/user/cloudera/Practice/doc1.csv'
   USING PigStorage(',') as (name:chararray,
   id:int,exp:int,hosp:chararray,fees:int);

pat1 = LOAD '/user/cloudera/Practice/pat1.csv'
   USING PigStorage(',') as (pid:int,pname:
   chararray,age:int,place:chararray,docid:int);

grunt> describe doc1;
doc1: {name: chararray,id: int,exp: int,hosp:
   chararray,fees: int}

grunt> describe pat1;
pat1: {pid: int,pname: chararray,age: int,place:
   chararray,docid: int}
```

Q) Display the details of all doctor across various hospitals in the dataset with their corresponding patient details.

```
grunt> lj = join doc1 by id left,pat1 by docid; (OR)
grunt> lj = join doc1 by id left outer,pat1 by
   docid;
grunt> dump lj;
```

```
(Milan,1001,5,apollo,500,,,,,)
(Jay,1002,10,apollo,500,,,,,)
(Lalit,1003,20,manipal,500,106,chaitanya,30,
    belandur,1003)
(Mohit,1004,15,Columbia,600,107,nani,27,
    krpuram,1004)
(Mohit,1004,15,Columbia,600,104,tarun,25,
    HSR,1004)
(Mohit,1004,15,Columbia,600,101,harinath,5,
    domlur,1004)
(Chauhan,1005,30,narayana,550,102,nagarjun,10,
    varthur,1005)
(Suraj,1006,25,manipal,650,105,prabas,15,
    marthahalli,1006)
(Suraj,1006,25,manipal,650,103,chirajeevi,20,
    HAL,1006)
(Jayanth,1007,13,apollo,550,,,,,)
```

Right Outer Join

The right outer join operation returns all rows from the right table, even if there are no matches in the left table.

Q) Display the details of all patients those who have already visited and those who are yet to take appointment along with their corresponding doctor details.

```
grunt> lj = join doc1 by id right,pat1 by docid;
```
                                                              (OR)
```
grunt> lj = join doc1 by id right outer,
    pat1 by docid;

grunt> rj;
```

```
OUTPUT:
(Lalit,1003,20,manipal,500,106,chaitanya,30,
    belandur,1003)
(Mohit,1004,15,Columbia,600,107,nani,27,
    krpuram,1004)
```

```
(Mohit,1004,15,Columbia,600,104,tarun,25,
   HSR,1004)
(Mohit,1004,15,Columbia,600,101,harinath,5,
   domlur,1004)
(Chauhan,1005,30,narayana,550,102,nagarjun,10,
   varthur,1005)
(Suraj,1006,25,manipal,650,105,prabas,15,
   marthahalli,1006)
(Suraj,1006,25,manipal,650,103,chirajeevi,20,
   HAL,1006)
(,,,,,109,karthik,10,varthur,)
(,,,,,108,varun,23,HSR,)
```

6.8 COMBINING & SPLITTING – UNION, SPLIT

6.8.1 Union Operator

The **UNION** operator of Pig Latin is used to merge the content of two relations. To perform UNION operation on two relations, their columns and domains must be identical.

```
Syntax:
grunt> Relation_name3 = UNION Relation_name1,
   Relation_name2;
```

Assume two files for joining as:

```
doctor.csv
Milan,1001,5,apollo,500
Jay,1002,10,apollo,500
lalit,1003,20,manipal,500
Mohit,1004,15,columbia,600
Chauhan,1005,30,narayana,550
Suraj,1006,25,manipal,650

d.csv
meena,2001,20,rxdx,650
leena,2001,15,st johns,450
sonam,2002,30,rxdx,600
```

```
doc = LOAD '/user/cloudera/Practice/doctor.csv'
    USING PigStorage(',') as
    (name:chararray,id:int,exp:int,hosp:chararray,
    fees:int);

grunt> doc1 = LOAD '/user/cloudera/Practice/d.csv'
    USING  PigStorage(',') as
    (name:chararray,id:int,exp:int,hosp:chararray,
    fees:int);
grunt> dump doc1;
```

```
(meena,2001,20,rxdx,650)
(leena,2001,15,st johns,450)
(sonam,2002,30,rxdx,600)
```

```
grunt> result = union doc,doc1;
grunt> dump result;
```

```
OUTPUT:
(Milan,1001,5,apollo,500)
(Jay,1002,10,apollo,500)
(lalit,1003,20,manipal,500)
(Mohit,1004,15,columbia,600)
(Chauhan,1005,30,narayana,550)
(Suraj,1006,25,manipal,650)
(,,,,)
(meena,2001,20,rxdx,650)
(leena,2001,15,st johns,450)
(sonam,2002,30,rxdx,600)
```

6.8.2 Split Operator

The **SPLIT** operator is used to split a relation into two or more relations.

```
Syntax:
grunt> SPLIT   Relation_name INTO Relation2_name
    IF (condition1), Relation2_name (condition2);
```

```
grunt> split doc into senior if exp>15,junior if
    (exp>5 and exp<=15);
grunt> dump senior;
```

```
OUTPUT:
(lalit,1003,20,manipal,500)
(Chauhan,1005,30,narayana,550)
(Suraj,1006,25,manipal,650)
```

```
(lalit,1003,20,manipal,500)
(Chauhan,1005,30,narayana,550)
(Suraj,1006,25,manipal,650)
```

```
grunt> dump junior;
```

```
OUTPUT:
(Jay,1002,10,apollo,500)
(Mohit,1004,15,columbia,600)
```

6.9 SORTING – ORDER, LIMIT, RANK

6.9.1 Order – By Operator

The **ORDER BY** operator is used to display the contents of a relation in a sorted order based on one or more fields. By default, the ordering happens in ascending order.

```
Syntax:
grunt> Relation_name2 = ORDER Relatin_name BY
    (ASC|DESC);
```

Q) Display the details of doctor in ascending order of their name.

```
grunt> a = order doc by name asc;              (OR)
grunt> a = order doc by name;
grunt> dump a;
```

```
OUTPUT:
(Chauhan,1005,30,narayana,550)
(Jay,1002,10,apollo,500)
(Milan,1001,5,apollo,500)
(Mohit,1004,15,columbia,600)
(Suraj,1006,25,manipal,650)
(lalit,1003,20,manipal,500)    //lowercase 'l' is
                                 ordered after all
                                 uppercase letters
```

Q) Display the details of doctor in ascending order of fees amount and if there is a tie, then it broken using experience in descending order.

```
grunt> a= order doc by fees asc,exp desc;        (OR)
grunt> a= order doc by $4 asc,$2 desc;
grunt> dump a;
```

```
OUTPUT:
(Lalit,1003,20,manipal,500)
(Jay,1002,10,apollo,500)
(Milan,1001,5,apollo,500)
(Chauhan,1005,30,narayana,550)
(Mohit,1004,15,Columbia,600)
(Suraj,1006,25,manipal,650)
```

6.9.2 Limit Operator

The **LIMIT** operator is used to get a limited number of tuples from a relation.

```
Syntax:
grunt> Result = LIMIT Relation_name number_of_
    tuples;
```

```
grunt> a = limit doc 2;
grunt> dump a;
```

```
OUTPUT:
(Jay,1002,10,apollo,500)
(Milan,1001,5,apollo,500)
```

Q) Display the doctor id, doctor name, experience of first 3 highest experienced doctor details from 'Apollo' or 'Manipal' hospital.

```
grunt> a = filter doc by hosp=='apollo' or
    hosp=='manipal';
grunt> describe a;
grunt> a1 = foreach a generate name,id,exp;
grunt> a2 = order a1 by exp desc;
grunt> a3 = limit a2 3;
```

```
OUTPUT:
(Suraj,1006,25)
(Lalit,1003,20)
(Jay,1002,10)
```

6.9.3 Rank Operator

RANK operator simply prepends a sequential value to each tuple when no field is specified to sort. Otherwise, the RANK operator uses each field (or set of fields) to sort the relation. The rank of a tuple is one plus the number of different rank values preceding it. If two or more tuples tie on the sorting field values, they will receive the same rank.

NOTE: When using the option **DENSE**, ties do not cause gaps in ranking values.

```
grunt> a = RANK doc by fees desc;
grunt> dump a;
```

```
OUTPUT:
(1,Suraj,1006,25,manipal,650)
(2,Mohit,1004,15,Columbia,600)
(3,Chauhan,1005,30,narayana,550)
(4,Lalit,1003,20,manipal,500)
(4,Jay,1002,10,apollo,500)
(4,Milan,1001,5,apollo,500)
```

Same example as previous, but DENSE. In this case there are no gaps in ranking values. Here when fees are same, then tie is broken with experience in descending order and ranks are assigned based on that.

```
grunt> a = RANK doc by fees desc,exp desc dense;
grunt> dump a;
```

```
OUTPUT:
(1,Suraj,1006,25,manipal,650)
(2,Mohit,1004,15,Columbia,600)
(3,Chauhan,1005,30,narayana,550)
(4,Lalit,1003,20,manipal,500)
(5,Jay,1002,10,apollo,500)
(6,Milan,1001,5,apollo,500)
```

6.10 TYPE CONSTRUCTION OPERATOR

Description

Operator	Symbol	Notes
tuple constructor	( )	Use to construct a tuple from the specified elements.
bag constructor	{ }	Use to construct a bag from the specified elements
map constructor	[ ]	Use to construct a map from the specified elements.

Tuple Construction

```
grunt> a = foreach doc generate name,id,exp;
grunt> dump a;
```

```
OUTPUT:
(Milan,1001,5)
(Jay,1002,10)
(lalit,1003,20)
(Mohit,1004,15)
(Chauhan,1005,30)
(Suraj,1006,25)
```

Bag Construction

```
grunt> a =foreach doc generate { (name,id,exp) },
    {name,id,exp};
grunt> dump a;
```

```
OUTPUT:
({ (Milan,1001,5) },{ (Milan), (1001), (5) })
({ (Jay,1002,10) },{ (Jay), (1002), (10) })
({ (lalit,1003,20) },{ (lalit), (1003), (20) })
({ (Mohit,1004,15) },{ (Mohit), (1004), (15) })
({ (Chauhan,1005,30) },{ (Chauhan), (1005), (30) })
({ (Suraj,1006,25) },{ (Suraj), (1006), (25) })
```

Map Construction

```
grunt> a = foreach doc generate [name,exp];
grunt> dump a;
```

```
OUTPUT:
([Milan#5])
([Jay#10])
([lalit#20])
([Mohit#15])
([Chauhan#30])
([Suraj#25])
([null#])
```

6.11 NULL OPERATORS AND FLATTEN OPERATOR

NULL Operator

The two null operators are:

- is null

- is not null

```
Example:
grunt> a = filter doc by hosp is not null;
grunt> dump a;
```

```
OUTPUT:
(Milan,1001,5,apollo,500)
(Jay,1002,10,apollo,500)
(Lalit,1003,20,manipal,500)
(Mohit,1004,15,Columbia,600)
(Chauhan,1005,30,narayana,550)
(Suraj,1006,25,manipal,650)
```

Flatten Operator

It changes the structure of tuples and bags. Flatten un-nests tuples, bags and maps.

Consider the below 'num' file stored on HDFS

```
$gedit num
1,2,3
4,5,6
7,8,9
10,11,12
13,14,15

$hadoop fs -put num /user/cloudera/Practice
```

For tuples, flatten substitutes the fields of a tuple in place of the tuple. Let see the below example:

```
grunt> a = foreach num generate f1,(f2,f3);
grunt> dump a;
```

```
(1,(2,3))
(4,(5,6))
(7,(8,9))
(10,(11,12))
(13,(14,15))
```

```
grunt> res = foreach a generate $0, flatten($1);
grunt> dump res;
```

```
OUTPUT:
(1,2,3)
(4,5,6)
(7,8,9)
(10,11,12)
(13,14,15)
```

For bags, when flatten operator is used to un-nest a bag, new tuples are created. Refer the below example, where on apply of GENERATE flatten ($0), we end up with two tuples.

```
grunt> a = foreach num generate { (f1,f3), (f1,f2) };
grunt> dump a;
```

```
({(1,3),(1,2)})
({(4,6),(4,5)})
({(7,9),(7,8)})
({(10,12),(10,11)})
({(13,15),(13,14)})
```

```
grunt> res = foreach a generate flatten($0);
grunt> dump res;
```

```
OUTPUT:
(1,3)
(1,2)
(4,6)
(4,5)
(7,9)
(7,8)
(10,12)
(10,11)
(13,15)
(13,14)
```

When the flatten operator is used to remove a level of nesting in a bag, then sometimes it leads to a cross product action. For example, consider the below relation that has a tuple of the form (a, {(b,c), (d,e)}), commonly produced by the GROUP operator. If we apply the expression GENERATE $0, flatten ($1) to this tuple, we will create new tuples: (a, b, c) and (a, d, e).

```
grunt> a = foreach num generate f1,{(f1,f3),
    (f1,f2)};
grunt> dump a;
(1,{(1,3),(1,2)})
(4,{(4,6),(4,5)})
(7,{(7,9),(7,8)})
(10,{(10,12),(10,11)})
(13,{(13,15),(13,14)})
grunt> res = foreach a generate $0,flatten($1);
grunt> dump res;
```

```
OUTPUT:
(1,1,3)
(1,1,2)
(4,4,6)
(4,4,5)
(7,7,9)
(7,7,8)
(10,10,12)
(10,10,11)
(13,13,15)
(13,13,14)
```

6.12 EVAL BUILT_IN FUNCTIONS

AVG( ), MIN( ), MAX( ), SUM( )

The Pig-Latin AVG(), MIN(), MAX(), SUM() functions are used to compute the average, minimum, maximum, total of the numerical values within a bag. While calculating these corresponding values, these functions ignores the NULL values.

Note –

- To get the global overall value, we need to perform a Group All operation, and calculate the average, minimum, maximum, total values using the AVG(), MIN(), MAX(), SUM() function respectively.

- To get the average, minimum, maximum, total value of a group, we need to group it using the **Group By** operator and proceed with the average, minimum, maximum, total function respectively.

AVG()

Q) Display hospital name, fees and average fees among all the hospital.

```
grunt> dump gr
```

```
(Milan,1001,5,apollo,500)
(Jay,1002,10,apollo,500)
(lalit,1003,20,manipal,500)
(Mohit,1004,15,columbia,600)
(Chauhan,1005,30,narayana,550)
(Suraj,1006,25,manipal,650)
```

```
grunt> gr = group doc all;
grunt> describe gr;
```

> gr: {group: chararray,doc: {(name: chararray,
>   id: int,exp: int,hosp: chararray,fees: int)}}

```
grunt> dump gr;
```

> (all,{(Milan,1001,5,apollo,500),(Jay,1002,10,
>   Apollo,500),(lalit,1003,20,manipal,500),
>   (Mohit,1004,15,columbia,600),(Chauhan,1005,
>   30,narayana,550),(Suraj,1006,25,manipal,650)})

```
grunt> result = foreach gr generate
doc.hosp,doc.fees,AVG(doc.fees);
```

OUTPUT:
> ({(apollo),(apollo),(manipal),(columbia),
>   (narayana),(manipal),()},{(500),(500),(500),
>   (600),(550),(650),()},550.0)

MAX()

Q) Display hospital name, fees and maximum fees among all the hospital.

```
grunt> result = foreach gr generate doc.hosp,
   doc.fees,MAX(doc.fees);
grunt> dump result;
```

OUTPUT:
> ({(manipal),(narayana),(Columbia),(manipal),
>   (apollo),(apollo)},{(650),(550),(600),(500),
>   (500),(500)},650)

MIN()

Q) Display hospital name, fees and minimum fees among all the hospital.

```
grunt> result= foreach gr generate doc.hosp,
   doc.fees,MIN(doc.fees);
grunt> dump result;
```

```
OUTPUT:
({(apollo),(apollo),(manipal),(columbia),
   (narayana),(manipal),()},{(500),(500),
   (500),(600),(550),(650),()},500)
```

SUM()

Q) Display hospital name, fees and total fees among all the hospital.

```
grunt> result = foreach gr generate doc.hosp,
   doc.fees,SUM(doc.fees);
grunt> dump result;
```

```
OUTPUT:
({(apollo),(apollo),(manipal),(columbia),
   (narayana),(manipal),()},{(500),(500),(500),
   (600),(550),(650),()},3300)
```

COUNT( )

The COUNT() function of Pig Latin is used to get the number of elements in a bag. While counting the number of tuples in a bag, the COUNT() function ignores (will not count) the tuples having a NULL value in the FIRST FIELD.

The COUNT_STAR() function of Pig Latin is similar to the COUNT() function. It is used to get the number of elements in a bag. While counting the elements, the COUNT_STAR() function includes the NULL values.

Note –

- To get the global count value (total number of tuples in a bag), we need to perform a Group All operation, and calculate the count value using the COUNT() or COUNT_STAR() function.

- To get the count value of a group (Number of tuples in a group), we need to group it using the Group By operator and proceed with the count function.

Q) Display total no:of tuples/rows in relation.

```
grunt> result = foreach gr generate COUNT(doc.id);
grunt> dump result;
```

```
(6)
```

Assume the below dataset, loaded to HDFS and then loaded to PigStorage in mapreduce mode.

d.txt
```
meena,2001,20,rxdx,650
lalit,1003,20,manipal,500
leena,2001,15,st johns,450
Suraj,1006,25,manipal,650
jay,1002,10,apollo,500
,,,,,
,,,,,
```

grunt> dump d;
```
(meena,2001,20,rxdx,650)
(lalit,1003,20,manipal,500)
(leena,2001,15,st johns,450)
(Suraj,1006,25,manipal,650)
(jay,1002,10,apollo,500)
(,,,,)
(,,,,)
```

```
grunt> gr =group d all;
grunt> describe gr;
```

```
gr:{group:chararray,d:{(name:chararray,id:int,
    exp:int,hosp:chararray,fees:int)}}
```

```
grunt> result = foreach gr generate COUNT(d.id);
grunt> dump result;
```

```
OUTPUT:
(5)
```

```
grunt> result = foreach gr generate COUNT_STAR(d.id);
grunt> dump result;
```

```
OUTPUT:
(7)
```

SIZE()

The SIZE() function of Pig Latin is used to compute the number of elements based on any Pig data type.

Data Type	Value
int, long, float, double	For all these types, the size function returns 1.
Char array	For a char array, the size() function returns the number of characters in the array.
Tuple	For a tuple, the size() function returns number of fields in the tuple.
Bag	For a bag, the size() function returns number of tuples in the bag.
Map	For a map, the size() function returns the number of key/value pairs in the map.

Q) Display doctor name along with the length of doctor name in each row.

```
grunt> ans = foreach doc generate name,SIZE(name);
grunt> dump ans;
```

```
OUTPUT:
(Milan,5)
(Jay,3)
(lalit,5)
(Mohit,5)
(Chauhan,7)
(Suraj,5)
```

CONCAT( )

The **CONCAT()** function of Pig Latin is used to concatenate two or more expressions of the same type. If the datatypes of the fields in CONCAT() function are not chararray, then perform explicit typecast for concatenation.

```
Syntax:
grunt> CONCAT (expression, expression, [...
    expression])
```

Q) Display doctor name and hospital name as one word.

```
grunt> ans = foreach doc generate CONCAT(name,hosp);
grunt> dump ans;
```

OUTPUT:
```
(Milanapollo)
(Jayapollo)
(lalitmanipal)
(Mohitcolumbia)
(Chauhannarayana)
(Surajmanipal)
```

Q) Display doctor name and his/her experience as one word.

```
grunt> ans = foreach doc generate CONCAT(name,
   (chararray)exp);
grunt> dump ans;
```

OUTPUT:
```
(Milan5)
(Jay10)
(Lalit20)
(Mohit15)
(Chauhan30)
(Suraj25)
```

Q) Display doctor name and hospital name as one word separated by '@' symbol.

```
grunt> ans = foreach doc generate CONCAT
   (name,'@',hosp);
```

OUTPUT:
```
(Milan@apollo)
(Jay@apollo)
(Lalit@manipal)
(Mohit@Columbia)
(Chauhan@narayana)
(Suraj@manipal)
```

Q) Display doctor name and his/her experience as one word separated by '_' symbol.

```
grunt> ans = foreach doc generate
    CONCAT(name,'_',(chararray)exp);
grunt> dump ans;
```

```
OUTPUT:
(Milan_5)
(Jay_10)
(Lalit_20)
(Mohit_15)
(Chauhan_30)
(Suraj_25)
```

IsEmpty()

The `IsEmpty()` function of Pig Latin is used to check if a bag or map is empty.

Refer the following output from 6.7.2 Co-Group section

```
OUTPUT:
grunt> dump a;
(5,{(Milan,1001,5,apollo,500)},{(7006,anshul,
    5,chennai)})
(10,{(Jay,1002,10,apollo,500)},{(7001,ameena,
    10,bang),(7005,alester,10,hyd)})
(15,{(Mohit,1004,15,columbia,600)},{(7004,alen,
    15,hyd)})
(20,{(lalit,1003,20,manipal,500)},{(7002,amit,
    20,chennai)})
(25,{(Suraj,1006,25,manipal,650)},{})
(30,{(Chauhan,1005,30,narayana,550)},{(7003,
    anand,30,bang)})
```

Here. The second bad is empty for tuple grouped for experience 25.

```
grunt> describe a;
```

> *a: {group: int,doc: { (name: chararray,id:*
> *int,exp: int,hosp: chararray,fees: int)},emp:*
> *{ (id: int,name: chararray,exp: int,place:*
> *chararray)}}*

```
grunt> res = filter a by IsEmpty(emp);
grunt> dump res;
```

OUTPUT:
(25,{(Suraj,1006,25,manipal,650)},{})

TOKENIZE()

It is used to split a string (which contains a group of words) in a single tuple and returns a bag which contains the output of the split operation.

Syntax:
```
grunt> TOKENIZE(expression [, 'field_delimiter'])
```

As a delimeter to the **TOKENIZE()** function, we can pass space [ ], double quote [" "], coma [,], parenthesis [()], star [*]. Assume the below file stored in HDFS.

Example 1:
Split.txt
```
001,"naveen""bhatt",cse
002,rajesh"khanna",ise
003,(preeti)(agrwal),me
004,hello*world,cse
```

```
grunt> sp = load '/user/cloudera/Practice/
   split.txt' using PigStorage(',') as (id:int,
   name:chararray, dept:chararray);
grunt> dump sp;
```

> *(1,"naveen""bhatt",cse)*
> *(2,rajesh"khanna",ise)*
> *(3,(preeti)(agrwal),me)*
> *(4,hello*world,cse)*

```
grunt> result = foreach sp generate TOKENIZE(name);
grunt> dump result;
```

OUTPUT:
({(naveen),(bhatt)})
({(rajesh),(khanna)})
({(preeti),(agrwal)})
({(hello),(world)})

Example 2:
Split.txt
001,"naveen""bhatt",cse
002,rajesh"khanna",ise
003,(preeti)(agrwal),me
004,hello*world,cse
005,hello12356,ise
006,abcd12ghj,me
007,asd   dfg,ise

```
grunt> result = foreach sp generate TOKENIZE(name);
grunt> dump result;
```

OUTPUT:
({(naveen),(bhatt)})
({(rajesh),(khanna)})
({(preeti),(agrwal)})
({(hello),(world)})
({(hello12356)})
({(abcd12ghj)})
({(asd),(dfg)})

6.13 STRING BUILT_IN FUNCTIONS

SUBSTRING()

This function returns a substring from the given string.

This function accepts three parameters one is the column name of the string we want. And the other two are the start and stop indexes of the required substring.

```
Syntax:
grunt> SUBSTRING(string, startIndex, stopIndex)
```

Q) Display doctor id, name along with first two letter of doctor's name.

```
grunt> ans = foreach doc
    generate(id,name),SUBSTRING(name,0,2);
grunt> dump ans;
```

```
OUTPUT:
((1001,Milan),Mi)
((1002,Jay),Ja)
((1003,lalit),la)
((1004,Mohit),Mo)
((1005,Chauhan),Ch)
((1006,Suraj),Su)
```

```
Here,
0:starting index of search
2:ending position + 1
```

Q) Display doctor id, name along with 3rd letter of doctor's name.

```
grunt>ans = foreach doc generate(id,name),
    SUBSTRING(name,2,3);
grunt> dump ans;
```

```
OUTPUT:
((1001,Milan),l)
((1002,Jay),y)
((1003,lalit),l)
((1004,Mohit),h)
((1005,Chauhan),u)
((1006,Suraj),r)
```

STARTSWITH()

This function accepts two string parameters. It verifies whether the first string starts with the second parameter mentioned in the function.

Q) Display true if doctor's name starts with letter 'M' along with doctor id, name.

```
grunt> a = foreach doc generate (id,name),
    STARTSWITH(name,'M');
grunt> dump a;
```

```
OUTPUT:
((1001,Milan),true)
((1002,Jay),false)
((1003,Lalit),false)
((1004,Mohit),true)
((1005,Chauhan),false)
((1006,Suraj),false)
```

ENDSWITH()

This function accepts two String parameters, it is used to verify whether the first string ends with the second string mentioned in the function.

Q) Display true if doctor's name ends with letter 't' along with doctor name.

```
grunt> a = foreach doc generate name,
    ENDSWITH(name,'t');
grunt> dump a;
```

```
OUTPUT:
(Milan,false)
(Jay,false)
(Lalit,true)
(Mohit,true)
(Chauhan,false)
(Suraj,false)
```

INDEXOF()

This function accepts a string value, a character and an index (integer). It returns the first occurrence of the given character in the string, searching forward from the given index.

```
Syntax:
grunt> INDEXOF(string, 'character', startIndex)
```

Q) Display doctor id, name along with the position of first occurrence of letter 'a' in doctor's name.

```
grunt> ans = foreach doc generate
    (id,name),INDEXOF(name,'a',0);
grunt> dump ans;
```

```
OUTPUT:
((1001,Milan),3)
((1002,Jay),1)
((1003,lalit),1)
((1004,Mohit),-1)
((1005,Chauhan),2)
((1006,Suraj),3)
```

The above statement parses the name of each doctor and returns the index value at which the letter 'a' occurred for the first time. If the name doesn't contain the letter 'a' it returns the value -1

Q) Display doctor id, name along with the position of first occurrence of letter 'a' in doctor's name, starting search from 3rd letter.

```
grunt> ans = foreach doc generate
    (id,name),INDEXOF(name,'a',3);
grunt> dump ans;
```

```
OUTPUT:
((1001,Milan),3)
((1002,Jay),-1)
((1003,lalit),-1)
((1004,Mohit),-1)
((1005,Chauhan),5)
((1006,Suraj),3)
```

LCFIRST()

This function is used to convert the first character of the given string into lowercase.

```
grunt> ans = foreach doc generate (id,name),
    LCFIRST(name);
grunt> dump ans;
```

```
OUTPUT:
((1001,Milan),milan)
((1002,Jay),jay)
((1003,lalit),lalit)
((1004,Mohit),mohit)
((1005,Chauhan),chauhan)
((1006,Suraj),suraj)
```

UCFIRST()

This function accepts a string, converts the first letter of it into uppercase, and returns the result.

```
grunt> ans = foreach doc generate (id,hosp),
    UCFIRST(hosp);
grunt> dump ans;
```

```
OUTPUT:
((1001,apollo),Apollo)
((1002,apollo),Apollo)
((1003,manipal),Manipal)
((1004,columbia),Columbia)
((1005,narayana),Narayana)
((1006,manipal),Manipal)
```

UPPER()

This function is used to convert all the characters in a string to uppercase.

```
grunt> ans = foreach doc generate (id,name),
    UPPER(name);
grunt> dump ans;
```

```
OUTPUT:
((1001,Milan),MILAN)
((1002,Jay),JAY)
((1003,lalit),LALIT)
((1004,Mohit),MOHIT)
((1005,Chauhan),CHAUHAN)
((1006,Suraj),SURAJ)
```

LOWER()

This function is used to convert all the characters in a string to lowercase.

```
grunt> ans = foreach doc generate (id,name),
    LOWER(name);
grunt> dump ans;
```

> **OUTPUT:**
> *((1001,Milan),milan)*
> *((1002,Jay),jay)*
> *((1003,lalit),lalit)*
> *((1004,Mohit),mohit)*
> *((1005,Chauhan),chauhan)*
> *((1006,Suraj),suraj)*

REPLACE()

This function is used to replace all the characters in a given string with the new characters.

Syntax

This function accepts three parameters, namely,

- **string** – The string that is to be replaced. If we want to replace the string within a relation, we have to pass the column name the string belongs to.

- **regEXP** – Here we have to pass the string/regular expression we want to replace.

- **newChar** – Here we have to pass the new value of the string.

```
grunt> REPLACE(string, 'regExp', 'newChar');
```

Example 1:
```
grunt> ans = foreach doc generate
    (id,hosp),REPLACE(hosp,'apollo','appo');
grunt> dump ans;
```

```
OUTPUT:
((1001,apollo),appo)
((1002,apollo),appo)
((1003,manipal),manipal)
((1004,columbia),columbia)
((1005,narayana),narayana)
((1006,manipal),manipal)
```

Example 2:

```
grunt> ans = foreach doc generate (id,hosp),
    REPLACE(hosp,'llo','*');
grunt> dump ans;
```

```
OUTPUT:
((1001,apollo),apo*)
((1002,apollo),apo*)
((1003,manipal),manipal)
((1004,columbia),columbia)
((1005,narayana),narayana)
((1006,manipal),manipal)
```

6.14 BUILT_IN MATH FUNCTIONS

Assume the following sample dataset for Math Functions.

```
$gedit math.txt
5
16
9
2.5
2
3.5
3.14
-2.2
grunt> mat = load '/user/cloudera/Practice/math.
    txt' using PigStorage(',') as (data:float);
```

ABS():

The **ABS()** function of Pig Latin is used to calculate the absolute value of a given expression.

```
grunt> ans = foreach mat generate data,ABS(data);
grunt> dump ans;
```

```
OUTPUT:
(5.0,5.0)
(16.0,16.0)
(9.0,9.0)
(2.5,2.5)
(2.0,2.0)
(3.5,3.5)
(3.14,3.14)
(-2.2,2.2)
```

CBRT() : Cube Root

The **CBRT()** function of Pig Latin is used to calculate the cube root of a given expression.

```
grunt> ans = foreach mat generate data,CBRT(data);
grunt> dump ans;
```

```
OUTPUT:
(5.0,1.709975946676697)
(16.0,2.5198420997897464)
(9.0,2.080083823051904)
(2.5,1.3572088082974532)
(2.0,1.2599210498948732)
(3.5,1.5182944859378313)
(3.14,1.464344366810533)
(-2.2,-1.300591456247907)
```

SBRT() : Square Root

The **SQRT()** function of Pig Latin is used to calculate the square root of a given expression.

```
grunt> ans = foreach mat generate data,SQRT(data);
grunt> dump ans;
```

```
OUTPUT:
(5.0,2.23606797749979)
(16.0,4.0)
(9.0,3.0)
(2.5,1.5811388300841898)
(2.0,1.4142135623730951)
(3.5,1.8708286933869707)
(3.14,1.7720045442673602)
(-2.2,NaN)
```

COS():

The **COS()** function of Pig Latin is used to calculate the cosine value of a given expression (angle).

```
grunt> ans = foreach mat generate data,COS(data);
grunt> dump ans;
```

```
OUTPUT:
(5.0,0.28366218546322625)
(16.0,-0.9576594803233847)
(9.0,-0.9111302618846769)
(2.5,-0.8011436155469337)
(2.0,-0.4161468365471424)
(3.5,-0.9364566872907963)
(3.14,-0.99999873189461)
(-2.2,-0.5885011558074578)
```

SIN():

The **SIN()** function of Pig Latin is used to calculate the sine value of a given expression (angle)

```
grunt> ans = foreach mat generate data,SIN(data);
grunt> dump ans;
```

```
OUTPUT:
(5.0,-0.9589242746631385)
(16.0,-0.2879033166650653)
(9.0,0.4121184852417566)
(2.5,0.5984721441039564)
(2.0,0.9092974268256817)
(3.5,-0.35078322768961984)
(3.14,0.0015925480124451862)
(-2.2,-0.8084963757576692)
```

TAN():

The **TAN()** function of Pig Latin is used to calculate the tangent value of a given expression (angle)

```
grunt> ans = foreach mat generate data,TAN(data);
grunt> dump ans;
```

```
OUTPUT:
(5.0,-3.380515006246586)
(16.0,0.3006322420239034)
(9.0,-0.45231565944180985)
(2.5,-0.7470222972386603)
(2.0,-2.185039863261519)
(3.5,0.3745856401585947)
(3.14,-0.0015925500319664656)
(-2.2,1.37382291908733)
```

CEIL():

The CEIL() function is used to calculate value of a given expression rounded up to the nearest integer.

```
grunt> ans = foreach mat generate data,CEIL(data);
grunt> dump ans;
```

```
OUTPUT:
(5.0,5.0)
(16.0,16.0)
(9.0,9.0)
(2.5,3.0)
(2.0,2.0)
(3.5,4.0)
(3.14,4.0)
(-2.2,-2.0)
```

FLOOR():

The **FLOOR()** function is used to calculate the value of an expression rounded down to the nearest integer Here is the syntax of the **FLOOR()** function.

```
grunt> ans = foreach mat generate data,FLOOR(data);
grunt> dump ans;
```

```
OUTPUT:
(5.0,5.0)
(16.0,16.0)
(9.0,9.0)
(2.5,2.0)
(2.0,2.0)
(3.5,3.0)
(3.14,3.0)
(-2.2,-3.0)
```

EXP():

The **EXP()** function of Pig Latin is used to get the Euler's number **e** raised to the power of **x** (given expression).

```
grunt> ans = foreach mat generate data,FLOOR(data);
grunt> dump ans;
```

```
OUTPUT:
(5.0,148.4131591025766)
(16.0,8886110.520507872)
(9.0,8103.083927575384)
```

```
(2.5,12.182493960703473)
(2.0,7.38905609893065)
(3.5,33.11545195869231)
(3.14,23.103869282414397)
(-2.2,0.1108031530788277)
```

ROUND():

The **ROUND()** function is used to get the value of an expression rounded to an integer (if the result type is float) or rounded to a long (if the result type is double).

```
grunt> ans = foreach mat generate data,ROUND(data);
grunt> dump ans;
```

```
OUTPUT:
(5.0,5)
(16.0,16)
(9.0,9)
(2.5,3)
(2.0,2)
(3.5,4)
(3.14,3)
(-2.2,-2)
```

LOG10():

The **LOG10()** function of Pig Latin is used to calculate the natural logarithm base 10 value of a given expression.

```
grunt> ans = foreach mat generate data,LOG10(data);
grunt> dump ans;
```

```
OUTPUT:
(5.0,0.6989700043360189)
(16.0,1.2041199826559248)
(9.0,0.9542425094393249)
(2.5,0.3979400086720376)
(2.0,0.3010299956639812)
(3.5,0.5440680443502757)
(3.14,0.4969296625825472)
(-2.2,NaN)
```

LOG():

The **LOG()** function of Pig Latin is used to calculate the natural logarithm (base **e**) value of a given expression.

```
grunt> ans = foreach mat generate data,LOG(data);
grunt> dump ans;
```

```
OUTPUT:
(5.0,1.6094379124341003)
(16.0,2.772588722239781)
(9.0,2.1972245773362196)
(2.5,0.9162907318741551)
(2.0,0.6931471805599453)
(3.5,1.252762968495368)
(3.14,1.1442228333291342)
(-2.2,NaN)
```

Apache Pig – Running Scripts

COMMENTS IN PIG SCRIPT

While writing a script in a file, we can include comments in it as shown below.

Multi-line comments

We will begin the multi-line comments with '/*', end them with '*/'.

```
/* These are the multi-line comments
   In the pig script */
```

Single –line comments

We will begin the single-line comments with '--'.

```
--we can write single line comments like this.
```

Executing Pig Script in Batch mode

While executing Apache Pig statements in batch mode, follow the steps given below.

Step 1

Write all the required Pig Latin statements in a single file. We can write all the Pig Latin statements and commands in a single file and save it as **.pig** file.

Step 2

Execute the Apache Pig script. You can execute the Pig script from the shell (Linux) as shown below.

```
$ pig Sample_script.pig
```

7.1 SCRIPT FOR FINDING COUNT OF EACH WORD FROM A LARGE TEXT

Assume we have a file **text.csv** in HDFS '**/user/cloudera/Practice**' with the following content as sample. It can be any textbook chapters or very large text with any format.

```
$gedit text.csv
hai hello how are you
are you fine
the world is very beautiful....my name is om
my nation is INDIA
I live in bangalore....
I am fine..

$hadoop fs -put /home/cloudera/text.csv /user/
    cloudera/Practice
```

***Assume script file is created in same directory "/home/cloudera"**

```
$gedit count.pig
```

```
file = load '/user/cloudera/Practice/text.csv'as
    (line:chararray);
t = foreach file generate flatten(TOKENIZE(line))
    as word;
gr = group t by word;
wc = foreach gr generate group,COUNT(t.word);
final_wc = order wc by group;
dump final_wc;
store final_wc into'/user/cloudera/scriptwc' using
    PigStorage();
```

To run the script, use following command:

```
$pig count.pig
```

To verify whether output is stored in HDFS or not:

```
$hadoop fs -ls /user/cloudera/scriptwc
```

```
-rw-r--r-- 3 cloudera cloudera  171 2018-03-20
   01:41 /user/cloudera/scriptwc/part-r-00000
```

To Verify the Content of part file

```
$ hadoop fs -cat /user/cloudera/scriptwc/part*
```

OUTPUT:	
I	1
INDIA	1
am	1
and	1
are	2
bangalore....	1
beautiful....	1
fine	1
fine..	1
hai	1
hello	1
how	1
i	2
in	1
is	3
live	1
my	2
name	1
nation	1
om	1
the	1
very	1
world	1

7.1.1 EXECUTION OF ABOVE COUNT.PIG SCRIPT LINE BY LINE ON GRUNT SHELL

The first statement of the script will load the data in the file named **text. csv** as a relation named '**file**' with schema of line as chararray.

```
grunt>file = load '/user/cloudera/Practice/text.
    csv' as (line:chararray);
grunt> dump file;
```

```
(hai hello how are you)
(are you fine)
(the world is very beautiful....my name is om)
(my nation is INDIA)
(I live in bangalore....)
(I am fine..)

grunt> describe file;
file: {line: chararray}
```

In the next statement the content of '**file**' relation is tokenized as '**word**', here tokens are formed with respect to space in between and they are put in a bag for each row. This output is assigned to relation named '**t**'.

```
grunt> t = foreach file generate TOKENIZE(line) as
    word;
grunt> dump t;
```

```
({(hai),(hello),(how),(are),(you)})
({(are),(you),(fine)})
({(the),(world),(is),(very),(beautiful....),
    (my),(name),(is),(om)})
({(my),(nation),(is),(INDIA)})
({(i),(live),(in),(bangalore....)})
({(I),(am),(fine..)})
({(i),(and),(you)})
```

When flatten operator is applied on the above tokens, the corresponding tokens from each individual bag is un-nest out of the bag.

```
grunt>t = foreach file generate flatten(TOKENIZE(line))
    as word;
grunt>dump t;
```

```
(hai)
(hello)
(how)
(are)
(you)
```

```
(are)
(you)
(fine)
(the)
(world)
(is)
(very)
(beautiful....)
(my)
(name)
(is)
(om)
(my)
(nation)
(is)
(INDIA)
(i)
(live)
(in)
(bangalore....)
(I)
(am)
(fine..)
(i)
(and)
(you)
```

grunt> describe t;
```
t:{word: chararray}
```

Once the words are obtained as separate tokens from huge text dataset, then the next step is to group the similar words together to perform **count operation** on it.

```
gr = group t by word;
grunt> describe gr;
gr: {group: chararray,t:{(word: chararray)}}
grunt> dump gr;
```

```
(I, { (I) })
(i, { (i), (i) })
(am, { (am) })
(in, { (in) })
(is, { (is), (is), (is) })
(my, { (my), (my) })
(om, { (om) })
(and, { (and) })
(are, { (are), (are) })
(hai, { (hai) })
(how, { (how) })
(the, { (the) })
(you, { (you), (you), (you) })
(fine, { (fine) })
(live, { (live) })
(name, { (name) })
(very, { (very) })
(INDIA, { (INDIA) })
(hello, { (hello) })
(world, { (world) })
(fine.., { (fine..) })
(nation, { (nation) })
(bangalore...., { (bangalore....) })
(beautiful...., { (beautiful....) })
```

```
grunt> wc = foreach gr generate group,
   COUNT(t.word);                                    (OR)
grunt> wc = foreach gr generate group,COUNT(t);
grunt> describe wc;
```

```
wc: {group: chararray,long}
```

```
grunt> dump wc;
```

```
(I,1)
(i,2)
(am,1)
(in,1)
(is,3)
```

```
(my,2)
(om,1)
(and,1)
(are,2)
(hai,1)
(how,1)
(the,1)
(you,3)
(fine,1)
(live,1)
(name,1)
(very,1)
(INDIA,1)
(hello,1)
(world,1)
(fine..,1)
(nation,1)
(bangalore....,1)
(beautiful....,1)
```

The above output is ordered according to grouped word in ascending order

```
grunt> final_wc = order wc by group;
grunt> dump final_wc;
```

```
(I,1)
(INDIA,1)
(am,1)
(and,1)
(are,2)
(bangalore....,1)
(beautiful....,1)
(fine,1)
(fine..,1)
(hai,1)
(hello,1)
(how,1)
(i,2)
```

```
(in,1)
(is,3)
(live,1)
(my,2)
(name,1)
(nation,1)
(om,1)
(the,1)
(very,1)
(world,1)
(you,3)
```

7.2 SCRIPT TO COUNT NO: OF TIMES A PARTICULAR WORD IS REPEATED IN HUGE TEXT

```
$ gedit match.pig
```

```
file = load '/user/cloudera/pig_batc3/text.csv'
    using PigStorage() as (line:chararray);
token = foreach file generate
    flatten(TOKENIZE(line)) as word;
t = filter token by word matches 'you';
gr = group t by word;
wc = foreach gr generate group,COUNT(t.word);
final_wc = order wc by group;
dump final_wc;
store final_wc into '/user/cloudera/scriptgrep'
    using PigStorage();
```

To run the script, use following command:

```
$pig match.pig
```

To verify whether output is stored in newly created directory or not

```
$ hadoop fs -ls  /user/cloudera/scriptgrep
```

```
-rw-r--r--  3 cloudera cloudera  6 2018-03-20
    02:33 /user/cloudera/scriptgrep/part-r-00000
```

To verify the stored output

```
$ hadoop fs -cat /user/cloudera/scriptgrep/part*
```

```
OUTPUT:
you    3
```

7.3 WORKING WITH ONLINE SOCIAL NETWORKS DATA

Assume twitter dataset is in the form USER_ID \t FOLLOWER_ID \n where USER_ID and FOLLOWER_ID are represented by numeric ID (integer)

```
Example:
12     13
12     14
12     15
16     17
```

- *Users 13, 14 and 15 are followers of user 12.*
- *User 17 is a follower of user 16.*

Counting The Number of "Followers" Per Twitter User

Problem Statement:

For each user, calculate the total number of followers of that user. In the above example, user 12 has 3 followers and user 16 has 1 follower. The output will be as shown below:

```
USER_ID  \t  No. of FOLLOWERs \n
```

```
Example:
12   3
16   1
```

> **Follower Distribution:** For each user ID, count the number of users he/she follows.
>
> **Outliers Detection:** find outliers (users that have a number of followers above an arbitrary threshold — which you have to manually set,). Assume threshold is 3 in the below script.

To Create input file tweet.txt in localfile system and then copy it on HDFS (location: '/user/cloudera/Practice')

```
grunt> data = load '/user/cloudera/Practice/
   tweet.txt' using PigStorage(' ') as
   (id:chararray,fr:chararray);
grunt> dump data;
```

```
(TW 1, TW 3)
(TW 1, TW 8)
(TW 2, TW 1)
(TW 2, TW 3)
(TW 3, TW 1)
(TW 3, TW 5)
(TW 3, TW 7)
(TW 4, TW 5)
(TW 4, TW 6)
(TW 4, TW 7)
(TW 5, TW 3)
(TW 5, TW 4)
(TW 5, TW 8)
(TW 6, TW 1)
(TW 6, TW 4)
(TW 7, TW 2)
(TW 7, TW 8)
(TW 8, TW 1)
(TW 8, TW 5)
(TW 8, TW 7)
(TW 12,)
(,TW13)
```

***Assume script file is created in same directory "/home/cloudera"**

$ gedit tweet.pig

```
Data = load '/user/cloudera/Practice/tweet.txt' using
   PigStorage(' ') as (id:chararray,fr:chararray);
split data into good_data if id is not null and fr
   is not null,bad_data otherwise;
set1 = group good_data by id;
```

```
friends = foreach set1 generate group,COUNT(good_
   data.fr) as followers;
friends = order friends by group asc;
outliers = filter friends by followers<3;
set2 = group good_data by fr;
following_friends = foreach set2 generate
   group,COUNT(good_data.id) as followings;
following_friends = order following_friends by
   group asc;
store friends into '/user/cloudera/followers';
store following_friends into '/user/cloudera/pig_
   batc3/followings';
store outliers into '/user/cloudera/outliers';
```

To verify whether output is stored in HDFS or not:

```
$hadoop fs -ls /user/cloudera/
```

```
drwxr-xr-x  - cloudera cloudera  0 2018-03-20 03:54
   /user/cloudera/pig_batc3/followers
drwxrwxrwx  - cloudera cloudera  0 2018-03-20 03:54
   /user/cloudera/pig_batc3/followings
drwxrwxrwx  - cloudera cloudera  0 2018-03-20 03:54
   /user/cloudera/pig_batc3/outliers
```

To Verify the output of followers directory

```
$ hadoop fs -cat /user/cloudera/pig_batc3/
   followers/part*
```

```
OUTPUT:
TW1    2
TW2    2
TW3    3
TW4    3
TW5    3
TW6    2
TW7    2
TW8    3
```

To Verify the output of following directory

```
$ hadoop fs -cat /user/cloudera/pig_batc3/
    followings/part*
```

```
OUTPUT:
TW1    4
TW2    1
TW3    3
TW4    2
TW5    3
TW6    1
TW7    3
TW8    3
```

To Verify the output of outlier directory

```
$ hadoop fs -cat /user/cloudera/pig_batc3/outliers/
    part*
```

```
OUTPUT:
TW1    2
TW2    2
TW6    2
TW7    2
```

7.3.1 Execution of Above Tweet.Pig Script Line By Line on Grunt Shell

```
grunt> split data into good_data if id is not null
    and fr is not null,bad_data otherwise;
grunt> dump good_data;
```

```
(TW 1,  TW 3)
(TW 1,  TW 8)
(TW 2,  TW 1)
(TW 2,  TW 3)
(TW 3,  TW 1)
(TW 3,  TW 5)
(TW 3,  TW 7)
(TW 4,  TW 5)
```

```
(TW 4,  TW 6)
(TW 4,  TW 7)
(TW 5,  TW 3)
(TW 5,  TW 4)
(TW 5,  TW 8)
(TW 6,  TW 1)
(TW 6,  TW 4)
(TW 7,  TW 2)
(TW 7,  TW 8)
(TW 8,  TW 1)
(TW 8,  TW 5)
(TW 8,  TW 7)
```

grunt> dump bad_data;

```
(TW 12,)
(, TW 13)
```

grunt> set1 = group good_data by id;
grunt> describe set1;

```
set1: {group: chararray,good_data: {(id: chararray,
    fr: chararray)}}
```

grunt> dump set1;

```
(TW 1,{( TW 1,  TW 3),( TW 1,  TW 8)})
(TW 2,{( TW 2,  TW 1),( TW 2,  TW 3)})
(TW 3,{( TW 3,  TW 1),( TW 3,  TW 5),( TW 3,  TW 7)})
(TW 4,{( TW 4,  TW 5),( TW 4,  TW 6),( TW 4,  TW 7)})
(TW 5,{( TW 5,  TW 3),( TW 5,  TW 4),( TW 5,  TW 8)})
(TW 6,{( TW 6,  TW 1),( TW 6,  TW 4)})
(TW 7,{( TW 7,  TW 2),( TW 7,  TW 8)})
(TW 8,{( TW 8,  TW 1),( TW 8,  TW 5),( TW 8,  TW 7)})
```

grunt> friends = foreach set1 generate
    group,COUNT(good_data.fr);

grunt> describe friends;

```
friends: {group: chararray,long}
```

```
grunt> friends = foreach set1 generate
   group,COUNT(good_data.fr) as followers;
grunt> describe friends;
```

```
friends: {group: chararray,followers: long}
```

```
grunt> dump friends;
```

```
(TW1,2)
(TW2,2)
(TW3,3)
(TW4,3)
(TW5,3)
(TW6,2)
(TW7,2)
(TW8,3)
```

```
grunt> outliers = filter friends by followers<3;
grunt> se21 = group good_data by fr;
grunt> describe set2;
```

```
set2: {group: chararray,good_data: {(id:
   chararray,fr: chararray)}}
```

```
grunt> following_friends = foreach set2 generate
   group,COUNT(good_data.id) as followings;
grunt> describe following_friends;
```

```
following_friends: {group: chararray,followings:
   long}
```

```
grunt> dump following_friends;
```

```
(TW1,4)
(TW2,1)
(TW3,3)
(TW4,2)
(TW5,3)
(TW6,1)
(TW7,3)
(TW8,3)
```

7.4 WEB LOG RESULT ANALYSIS

The log reports contain time-stamped details of requested links, IP address, URL, status. The data is comma separated. Usually the scale of these datasets is quite huge and running queries in a conventional method is not possible. We count the total number of requests received from a specific IP address which gives us the number of visits by the user. For this statistic, we need to first aggregate the data based upon the IP address and then count the number of events/logs in that collection. we want to calculate statistics for only the requests which were successful i.e; requests with response code or status equal to 200.

To Create input file weblog.csv in localfile system and then copy it on HDFS (location: '/user/cloudera/Practice')

```
$ gedit weblog.csv
$ Hadoop fs -put weblog.csv /user/cloudera/Practice
```

```
Sample Input
10.128.2.1,[29/Nov/2017:06:58:55,GET /login.php
    HTTP/1.1,200
10.128.2.1,[29/Nov/2017:06:59:02,POST /process.php
    HTTP/1.1,302
10.128.2.1,[29/Nov/2017:06:59:03,GET /home.php
    HTTP/1.1,200
10.131.2.1,[29/Nov/2017:06:59:04,GET /js/vendor/
    moment.min.js HTTP/1.1,200
10.130.2.1,[29/Nov/2017:06:59:06,GET /
    bootstrap-3.3.7/js/bootstrap.js HTTP/1.1,200
10.130.2.1,[29/Nov/2017:06:59:19,GET /profile.
    php?user=bala HTTP/1.1,200
10.128.2.1,[29/Nov/2017:06:59:19,GET /js/jquery.
    min.js HTTP/1.1,200

10.131.2.1,[29/Nov/2017:06:59:19,GET /js/chart.
    min.js HTTP/1.1,200
10.131.2.1,[29/Nov/2017:06:59:30,GET /edit.
    php?name=bala HTTP/1.1,200
10.131.2.1,[29/Nov/2017:06:59:37,GET /logout.php
    HTTP/1.1,302
10.131.2.1,[29/Nov/2017:06:59:37,GET /login.php
    HTTP/1.1,200
```

```
10.130.2.1,[29/Nov/2017:07:00:19,GET /login.php
   HTTP/1.1,200
10.130.2.1,[29/Nov/2017:07:00:21,GET /login.php
   HTTP/1.1,200
10.130.2.1,[29/Nov/2017:13:31:27,GET / HTTP/
   1.1,302
10.130.2.1,[29/Nov/2017:13:31:28,GET /login.php
   HTTP/1.1,200
10.129.2.1,[29/Nov/2017:13:38:03,POST /process.php
   HTTP/1.1,302
10.131.0.1,[29/Nov/2017:13:38:04,GET /home.php
   HTTP/1.1,200
10.131.0.1,[29/Nov/2017:13:38:07,GET /contest
   problem.php?name=RUET%20OJ%20Server%20
   Testing%20Contest HTTP/1.1,200
10.130.2.1,[29/Nov/2017:13:38:19,GET / HTTP/
   1.1,302
10.131.2.1,[29/Nov/2017:13:38:20,GET /login.php
   HTTP/1.1,200
10.131.2.1,[29/Nov/2017:13:38:20,GET /css/
   bootstrap.min.css HTTP/1.1,200
10.128.2.1,[29/Nov/2017:13:38:20,GET /css/font-
   awesome.min.css HTTP/1.1,200
10.131.0.1,[29/Nov/2017:13:38:20,GET /css/
   normalize.css HTTP/1.1,200
10.128.2.1,[29/Nov/2017:13:38:20,GET /css/style.
   css HTTP/1.1,200
10.131.0.1,[29/Nov/2017:13:38:20,GET /js/vendor/
   modernizr-2.8.3.min.js HTTP/1.1,200
10.129.2.1,[29/Nov/2017:13:38:20,GET /css/main.css
   HTTP/1.1,200
```

***Assume script file is created in same directory "/home/cloudera"

$ **gedit web.pig**

```
log = LOAD '/user/cloudera/Practice/weblog.csv'
   USING PigStorage(',') as
   (ip:chararray,timest:chararray,url:
   chararray,status:int);
```

```
ok = filter log by status==200;
a = group ok by ip;
visits = foreach a generate group as Ip_addr,
    COUNT(ok) as total_visits;
sort_visit = rank visits by total_visits desc;
dump sort_visit;
store sort_visit into '/user/cloudera/web'
    using PigStorage();
```

To verify whether output is stored in HDFS or not:

```
$ hadoop fs -ls /user/cloudera
$ hadoop fs -ls /user/cloudera/web
```

To Verify the output of newly created directory

```
$ hadoop fs -cat /user/cloudera/web/p*
```

```
OUTPUT:
1   10.131.0.1     2961
2   10.128.2.1     2941
3   10.130.2.1     2895
4   10.129.2.1     1286
5   10.131.2.1     1247
```

Here, the total_visits to different URL by each IP address is counted and ranked according to highest count.

7.5 TO FIND MAXIMUM OCCURANCE OF 1ST LETTER

The aim is to split the whole text into words and then find out the first letter from each word. Later these first letter are grouped together to find out no: times each letter appears as the first letter in the entire text.

To Create input file about.txt in local file system and then copy it on HDFS (location: '/user/cloudera')

```
$ gedit about.txt
$ hadoop fs -put about.txt /user/cloudera
```

Apache Hadoop is a collection of open-source software utilities that facilitate using a network of many computers to solve problems involving massive amounts of data and computation. It provides a software framework for distributed storage and processing of big data using the MapReduce programming model. Originally designed for computer clusters built from commodity hardware still the common use, it has also found use on clusters of higher-end hardware. All the modules in Hadoop are designed with a fundamental assumption that hardware failures are common occurrences and should be automatically handled by the framework.

The core of Apache Hadoop consists of a storage part, known as Hadoop Distributed File System (HDFS), and a processing part which is a MapReduce programming model. Hadoop splits files into large blocks and distributes them across nodes in a cluster. It then transfers packaged code into nodes to process the data in parallel. This approach takes advantage of data locality, where nodes manipulate the data they have access to. This allows the dataset to be processed faster and more efficiently than it would be in a more conventional supercomputer architecture that relies on a parallel file system where computation and data are distributed via high-speed networking.

***Assume script file is created in same directory "/home/cloudera"**

$ gedit letter.pig

```
file = load '/user/cloudera/about.txt' using
    PigStorage() as (line:chararray);
token = foreach file generate flatten(TOKENIZE(line))
    as word;
t = foreach token generate SUBSTRING(word,0,1) as
    letter;
gr = group t by letter;
wc = foreach gr generate group,COUNT(t);
final_wc = order wc by $1 desc;
dump final_wc;
store final_wc into '/user/cloudera/occur' using
    PigStorage();
```

To verify whether output is stored in HDFS or not:

```
$ hadoop fs -ls /user/cloudera
$ hadoop fs -ls /user/cloudera/occur
```

To Verify the output of newly created directory

```
$ hadoop fs -cat /user/cloudera/occur/p*
```

```
OUTPUT:
a   52
t   34
c   29
i   27
o   24
p   24
H   22
f   20
s   17
m   16
A   15
d   15
b   15
u   13
w   10
h   9
n   7
l   7
T   7
M   7
S   7
.
.
.
.
```

7.6 TO FIND MAXIMUM OCCURANCE OF 1ST LETTER AS VOWELS AND CONSONANTS

The aim is to split the whole text into words and then find out the first letter from each word. Later these first letters are split into two relation: vowels and consonant. They are grouped separately in their respective relation to find out no: times each letter appears as the first letter in the entire text.

To Create input file about.txt in local file system and then copy it on HDFS (location: '/user/cloudera')

```
$ gedit about.txt
$ hadoop fs -put about.txt /user/cloudera
```

Apache Hadoop is a collection of open-source software utilities that facilitate using a network of many computers to solve problems involving massive amounts of data and computation. It provides a software framework for distributed storage and processing of big data using the MapReduce programming model. Originally designed for computer clusters built from commodity hardware still the common use, it has also found use on clusters of higher-end hardware. All the modules in Hadoop are designed with a fundamental assumption that hardware failures are common occurrences and should be automatically handled by the framework.

The core of Apache Hadoop consists of a storage part, known as Hadoop Distributed File System (HDFS), and a processing part which is a MapReduce programming model. Hadoop splits files into large blocks and distributes them across nodes in a cluster. It then transfers packaged code into nodes to process the data in parallel. This approach takes advantage of data locality, where nodes manipulate the data they have access to. This allows the dataset to be processed faster and more efficiently than it would be in a more conventional supercomputer architecture that relies on a parallel file system where computation and data are distributed via high-speed networking.

. . . .

***Assume script file is created in same directory "/home/cloudera"

```
$ gedit vc.pig
```

```
file = load '/user/cloudera/about.txt' using
    PigStorage() as (line:chararray);
token = foreach file generate
    flatten(TOKENIZE(line)) as word;
```

```
t = foreach token generate SUBSTRING(word,0,1) as
   letter;
lc = foreach t generate LOWER(letter);
split lc into vow if($0=='a' or $0=='e' or $0=='i'
   or $0=='0' or $0=='u'), cons otherwise;
gr_vow = group vow by $0;
gr_con = group cons by $0;
wc_vow = foreach gr_vow generate group,COUNT(vow);
wc_con = foreach gr_con generate group,COUNT(cons);
final_wc_vow = order wc_vow by $1 desc;
final_wc_con = order wc_con by $1 desc;
dump final_wc_vow;
dump final_wc_con;
store final_wc_vow into '/user/cloudera/cnt_vowel'
   using PigStorage();
store final_wc_con into '/user/cloudera/cnt_con'
   using PigStorage();
```

To verify whether output is stored in HDFS or not:

```
$ hadoop fs -ls /user/cloudera
$ hadoop fs -ls /user/cloudera/cnt_vowel
$ hadoop fs -ls /user/cloudera/cnt_con
```

To Verify the output of newly created directory

```
$ hadoop fs -cat /user/cloudera/cnt_vowel/p*
```

```
OUTPUT:
a   67
i   30
u   13
e   4
```

```
$ hadoop fs -cat /user/cloudera/cnt_con/p*
```

```
OUTPUT:
t    41
c    32
h    31
o    27
p    26
f    24
s    24
m    23
d    17
b    15
w    10
n    7
l    7
r    5
j    2
g    2
v    2
k    1
y    1
z    1
```

Chapter 8

Hive

8.1 INTRODUCTION

Hive is a data warehouse infrastructure tool to process structured data in Hadoop. It resides on top of Hadoop to summarize Big Data, and makes querying and analyzing easy.

Initially Hive was developed by Facebook, later the Apache Software Foundation took it up and developed it further as an open source under the name Apache Hive. It is used by different companies. For example, Amazon uses it in Amazon Elastic MapReduce.

Features of Hive

- It stores schema in a database and the data into HDFS.

- It is designed for OLAP.

- It provides SQL type language for querying called HiveQL or HQL (Hive Query Language).

- It is familiar, fast, scalable, and extensible.

- Hive supports any client application written in Java, PHP, Python, C++ or Ruby by exposing its Thrift server. (You can use these client – side languages embedded with SQL for accessing a database such as DB2, etc.).

- As the metadata information of Hive is stored in an RDBMS, it significantly reduces the time to perform semantic checks during query execution.

- But it is not a relational database.

- It is not good for sub-queries

- It not good for OnLine Transaction Processing (OLTP)

- It is not a language for real-time queries and row-level updates

Architecture of Hive

The following component diagram depicts the architecture of Hive:

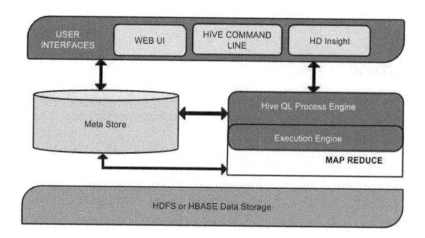

This component diagram contains different units. The following table describes each unit:

Unit Name	Operation
User Interface	Hive is a data warehouse infrastructure software that can create interaction between user and HDFS. The user interfaces that Hive supports are Hive Web UI, Hive command line, and Hive HD Insight (In Windows server).
Meta Store	Hive chooses respective database servers to store the schema or Metadata of tables, databases, columns in a table, their data types, and HDFS mapping.
HiveQL Process Engine	HiveQL is similar to SQL for querying on schema info on the Metastore. It is one of the replacements of traditional approach for MapReduce program. Instead of writing MapReduce program in Java, we can write a query for MapReduce job and process it.

Unit Name	Operation
Execution Engine	The conjunction part of HiveQL process Engine and MapReduce is Hive Execution Engine. Execution engine processes the query and generates results as same as MapReduce results. It uses the flavor of MapReduce.
HDFS or HBASE	Hadoop distributed file system or HBASE are the data storage techniques to store data into file system.

Data Models of HIVE

Databases: Namespaces function to avoid naming conflicts for tables, views, partitions, columns, and so on. Databases can also be used to enforce security for a user or group of users.

Tables: Homogeneous units of data which have the same schema. An example of a table could be **'student'** table, where each row could comprise of the following columns (schema):

- USN —which is of BIGINT type
- SNAME—which is of STRING type
- AGE-which is of INT type
- CITY—which is of STRING type
- DOJ-which is of TIMESTAMP

1. Managed Table:

As the name suggests (managed table), Hive is responsible for managing the data of a managed table. In other words, if you load the data from a file present in HDFS into a Hive Managed Table and issue a DROP command on it, the table along with its metadata will be deleted. So, the data belonging to the dropped managed_table no longer exist anywhere in HDFS and you can't retrieve it by any means. Basically, you are moving the data when you issue the LOAD command from the HDFS file location to the Hive warehouse directory.

> **Note!!!** The default path of the warehouse directory is set to/user/hive/ warehouse. The data of a Hive table resides in warehouse_directory/ table_name (HDFS). You can also specify the path of the warehouse directory in the hive.metastore.warehouse.dir configuration parameter present in the hive-site.xml.

2. External Table:

For external table, Hive is not responsible for managing the data. In this case, when you issue the LOAD command, Hive moves the data into its warehouse directory. Then, Hive creates the metadata information for the external table. Now, if you issue a DROP command on the external table, only metadata information regarding the external table will be deleted. Therefore, you can still retrieve the data of that external table from the warehouse directory using HDFS commands.

Partitions: Each Table can have one or more partition Keys which determines how the data is stored. Partitions—apart from being storage units—also allow the user to efficiently identify the rows that satisfy a specified criterion; for example, a date_partition of type STRING and country_partition of type STRING. Each unique value of the partition keys defines a partition of the Table.

For example, all students are partitioned year wise, then analysis on students of a particular batch can be done by referring only to that particular year partition.

Buckets (or **Clusters**): Data in each partition may in turn be divided into Buckets based on the value of a hash function of some column of the Table. For example, the "student" table may be bucketed by "city", which is one of the columns, other than the partitions columns, of the "student" table. These can be used to efficiently sample the data.

8.2 CONNECT TO HIVE

As Hive development has shifted from the original Hive server (HiveServer1) to the new server (HiveServer2), users and developers accordingly need to switch to the new client tool. However, there's more to this process than simply switching the executable name from "hive" to "beeline".

In its original form, Apache Hive was a heavyweight command-line tool that accepted queries and executed them utilizing MapReduce. Later, the tool was split into a client-server model, in which HiveServer1 is the server (responsible for compiling and monitoring MapReduce jobs) and Hive CLI is the command-line interface (sends SQL to the server).

Recently, the Hive community introduced HiveServer2 which is an enhanced Hive server designed for multi-client concurrency and improved authentication that also provides better support for clients connecting through JDBC and ODBC. Beeline is the CLI (command-line interface) developed specifically to interact with HiveServer2. It is based on the SQLLine CLI.

Now HiveServer2, with Beeline as the command-line interface, is the recommended solution; HiveServer1 and Hive CLI are deprecated and the latter won't even work with HiveServer2.

NOTE!!!
Before starting exercises on Hive, go to cloudera manager and check the health of 'Hive'. If its bad or not started yet, then start it from the action tab.

In Hive CLI interactive mode, you can execute any SQL query that is supported by HiveServer.

- **To start Hive CLI, Enter:**

```
$ hive
hive>
```

- **To start Beeline CLI, use the following commands:**

To start HiveServer2:
```
$ sudo service hive-server2 start
```

To stop HiveServer2:
```
$ sudo service hive-server2 stop
```

- The most important command to start beeline is 'connect command' to connect to a running HiveServer2 process. In this example the HiveServer2 process is running on localhost at port 10000:

- Hive specific commands (same as Hive CLI commands) can be run from Beeline, when the Hive JDBC driver is used. Use "; " (semicolon) to terminate commands. Comments in scripts can be specified using the "- -" prefix.

```
$ beeline
```

```
Beeline version 1.1.0-cdh5.13.0 by Apache Hive
```

```
beeline> show databases;
```

```
No current connection
```

```
beeline> !connect jdbc:hive2://localhost:10000
```

```
scan complete in 6ms
Connecting to jdbc:hive2://localhost:10000
Enter username for jdbc:hive2://localhost:10000:
                                         cloudera
Enter password for jdbc:hive2://localhost:10000:
                                         ********
Connected to: Apache Hive (version 1.1.0-
   cdh5.13.0)
Driver: Hive JDBC (version 1.1.0-cdh5.13.0)
Transaction isolation: TRANSACTION_REPEATABLE_
   READ
```

```
0: jdbc:hive2://localhost:10000> show databases;
```

Here, while connecting Hive Server through Beeline, it will ask for username and password. As shown above, the username is entered as "cloudera" and password is also as "cloudera"

8.3 DDL COMMANDS

Assume the following two sample files describing about employees and departments of a company. The data is delimited using the sumbol '|'. These files created or loaded in local file system.

```
$ gedit emp.csv
```

```
1001|hari|d1|chennai|1986-12-10
1002|teja|d1|hyd|1987-01-21
1003|ram|d3|delhi|1986-02-11
1004|milind|d4|bang|1988-03-21
1005|jay|d2|bang|1988-03-22
1006|naveen|d4|hyd|1986-04-12
1007|naser|d1|hyd|1989-11-15
1008|rahul|d3|delhi|1990-12-23
1009|jay|d6|hyd|1988-07-19
```

$ gedit dept.csv

```
d1|research|A-block
d2|sales|A-block
d3|testing|B-block
d4|development|C-block
d5|HR|A-block
```

To load the files to HDFS's any directory ('batch') from local file system.

```
$ hadoop fs -mkdir /user/cloudera/batch
$ hadoop fs -put emp.csv /user/cloudera/batch
$ hadoop fs -put dept.csv /user/cloudera/batch
```

Login to HIVE through HIVE CLI or Beeline and analyze the data using following commands

TO CREATE DATABSE

```
hive> create database test;                        (OR)
hive> create database if not exists test;
```

TO LIST OUT DATABASES

```
hive> show databases;
```

TO DROP DATABSE

```
hive> drop database test;                          (OR)
hive> drop database if exists test;
```

```
hive> drop database test cascade;                    (OR)
hive> drop database if exists test cascade;
```

NOTE!!!!

1. [if exists] & [if not exists] doesn't show error if database already exists while creating time and database doesn't exists while dropping the same respectively.

   Without these options, errors displayed clearly.

2. If database is not empty and to drop the entire database along with corresponding tables, use cascade option in drop database command.

TO MAKE USE OF THE DATABASE

```
hive> use test;
```

Create Table Statement

Create Table is a statement used to create a table in Hive. The syntax and example are as follows:

Syntax

CREATE [TEMPORARY][EXTERNAL] TABLE [IF NOT EXISTS]
[db_name.] table_name
[(col_name data_type [COMMENT col_comment],...)]
[COMMENT table_comment]
[ROW FORMAT row_format]
[STORED AS file_format]

Example:

```
hive> create table emp(id int, name string, dept
   string, place string, dob string)> comment 'this
   is employee table'> row format delimited fields
   terminated by '|' lines terminated by '\n'> stored
   as textfile;
```

(OR) Type the Statement in Single Line

```
hive> create table emp(id int,name string,dept
   string,place string,dob string) comment 'this
   is employee table' row format delimited fields
   terminated by '|' lines terminated by '\n' stored
   as textfile;
hive> create table department(did string,dname
   string,block string) comment 'this is department
   table' row format delimited fields terminated by
   '|' lines terminated by '\n' stored as textfile;
```

> **NOTE!!! You can mention the table in both the following ways:**
> Hive> USE test;
> Hive> CREATE TABLE emp(.....) ....
> **(OR)**
> Hive> CREATE TABLE test.emp(......) ....

TO SEE THE LIST OF TABLES

```
hive> show tables;
```

TO SEE THE STRUCTURE OF A TABLE

```
hive> describe emp;
```

TO SEE THE STRUCTURE & METADATA INFORMATION OF TABLE

```
hive> describe formatted emp;
hive> show create table emp;
```

To Verify the tables created through browser

```
Click on "Hadoop→HDFS Namenode→Utilities→
   Browse the file system→\→user→hive→
   warehouse→test.db
```

Contents of directory /user/hive/warehouse/test.db

Goto : |/user/hive/warehouse/test.d| go

Go to parent directory

Name	Type	Size	Replication	Block Size	Modification Time	Permission	Owner	Group
department	dir				2018-04-09 23:38	rwxrwxrwt	cloudera	hive
emp	dir				2018-04-09 23:57	rwxrwxrwt	cloudera	hive

ALTER TABLE STATEMENT

It is used to alter a table in Hive.

Syntax

The statement takes any of the following syntaxes based on what attributes we wish to modify in a table.

```
ALTER TABLE name RENAME TO new_name
ALTER TABLE name ADD COLUMNS (col_spec[, col_spec
    ...])
ALTER TABLE name CHANGE column_name new_name new_
    type
ALTER TABLE name REPLACE COLUMNS (col_spec[, col_
    spec ...])
```

TO RENAME TABLE NAME

```
hive> alter table department rename to d;
hive> show tables;
```

```
OUTPUT:
d
emp
```

TO ADD ONE OR MORE COLUMNS TO THE TABLE

```
hive> alter table d add columns (estb_year int,
    rating smallint);
hive> describe d;
```

```
OUTPUT:
did          string
dname        string
block        string
estb_year    int
rating       smallint
```

TO CHANGE COLUMN NAME OR ITS DATATYPE OR BOTH

Here, the column 'rating' is changed to column 'rate' but the datatype remains the same.

```
hive> alter table d change rating rate string;
hive> describe d;
```

```
OUTPUT:
did    string
dname string
block string
estb_year   int
rate   string
```

Here, the column 'rate' with string datatype earlier is changed to bigint datatype but the column name remains the same.

```
hive> alter table d change rate rate bigint;
hive> describe d;
```

```
OUTPUT:
did string
dname string
block string
estb_year   int
rate   bigint
```

Here, the column 'rate' with bigint datatype earlier is changed to int datatype with new column name as 'star'.

```
$alter table d change rate star int;
```

```
OUTPUT:
did          string
dname        string
block        string
estb_year    int
star         int
```

TO REPLACE COLUMNS

The description of the table 'd' before using 'Replace' command as follows:

```
hive> describe d;
```

```
OUTPUT:
did          string
dname        string
block        string
estb_year    int
rate         bigint
```

To replace the above 5 column by 3 columns as shown below:

```
hive> alter table d replace columns(did string,
    dname string, block string);
hive> describe d;
```

```
OUTPUT:
did      string
dname    string
block    string
```

To replace the above 3 columns by 1 column as shown below:

```
hive> alter table d replace columns (block string);
hive> describe d;
```

```
OUTPUT:
block  string
```

```
hive> select * from d;
```

```
OUTPUT:
d1
d2
d3
d4
```

//if you do REPLACE again, you will get the columns again I,e replace
is not removing columns permanently

```
hive> alter table d replace columns(did string,dname
    string, block string);
hive> desc d;
```

```
OUTPUT:
did    string
dname string
block string
```

```
hive> select * from d;
```

```
OUTPUT:
d1 research      A-block
d2 sales         A-block
d3 testing       B-block
d4 development   C-block
d5 hr            A-block
```

TO DROP THE TABLE

```
hive> drop table if exists d;                    (OR)
hive> drop table d;
```

8.4 LOAD DATA FROM LOCAL FILESYSTEM OR HDFS

LOAD DATA STATEMENT

Generally, after creating a table in SQL, we can insert data using the Insert
statement. But in Hive, we can insert data using the LOAD DATA statement.

While inserting data into Hive, it is better to use LOAD DATA to store bulk records. There are two ways to load data: one is from local file system and second is from Hadoop file system.

Syntax

The syntax for load data is as follows:

```
LOAD DATA [LOCAL] INPATH 'filepath' [OVERWRITE]
   INTO TABLE  tablename
[PARTITION(partcol1=val1, partcol2=val2 ...)]
```

- LOCAL is identifier to specify the local path. It is optional.

- OVERWRITE is optional to overwrite the data in the table.

- PARTITION is optional used table is created with partitions.

LOAD FROM LOCAL FILESYSTEM

```
hive> load data local inpath '/home/cloudera/emp.
   csv' into table emp;
hive> select * from emp;
```

```
OUTPUT:
1001    hari      d1    chennai    1986-12-10
1002    teja      d1    hyd        1987-01-21
1003    ram       d3    delhi      1986-02-11
1004    milind    d4    bang       1988-03-21
1005    jay       d2    bang       1988-03-22
1006    naveen    d4    hyd        1986-04-12
1007    naser     d1    hyd        1989-11-15
1008    rahul     d3    delhi      1990-12-23
1009    jay       d6    hyd        1988-07-19
```

Verifying throgh browser

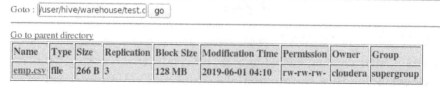

Contents of directory /user/hive/warehouse/test.db/emp

Goto : /user/hive/warehouse/test.d   go

Go to parent directory

Name	Type	Size	Replication	Block Size	Modification Time	Permission	Owner	Group
emp.csv	file	266 B	3	128 MB	2019-06-01 04:10	rw-rw-rw-	cloudera	supergroup

Go back to DFS home

LOAD FROM HADOOP FILE SYSTEM

```
hive> load data inpath '/user/cloudera/batch/emp.
   csv' into table emp;
hive> select * from emp;
```

OUTPUT:

```
1001    hari     d1   chennai   1986-12-10
1002    teja     d1   hyd       1987-01-21
1003    ram      d3   delhi     1986-02-11
1004    milind   d4   bang      1988-03-21
1005    jay      d2   bang      1988-03-22
1006    naveen   d4   hyd       1986-04-12
1007    naser    d1   hyd       1989-11-15
1008    rahul    d3   delhi     1990-12-23
1009    jay      d6   hyd       1988-07-19
1001    hari     d1   chennai   1986-12-10
1002    teja     d1   hyd       1987-01-21
1003    ram      d3   delhi     1986-02-11
1004    milind   d4   bang      1988-03-21
1005    jay      d2   bang      1988-03-22
1006    naveen   d4   hyd       1986-04-12
1007    naser    d1   hyd       1989-11-15
1008    rahul    d3   delhi     1990-12-23
1009    jay      d6   hyd       1988-07-19
```

Verifying through browser after loading from HDFS to 'emp' table

Contents of directory /user/hive/warehouse/test.db/emp

Goto : /user/hive/warehouse/test.d go

Go to parent directory

Name	Type	Size	Replication	Block Size	Modification Time	Permission	Owner	Group
emp.csv	file	266 B	3	128 MB	2019-06-01 04:10	rw-rw-rw-	cloudera	supergroup
emp_copy_1.csv	file	266 B	3	128 MB	2019-06-01 03:48	rw-rw-rw-	cloudera	cloudera

Go back to DFS home

> **NOTE!!!!**
> Since no overwrite keyword was used; the data got appended to same table 'emp' on load from HDFS. And in the directory '/user/hive/warehouse/test.db/emp', two copies of same content got generated.

TO LOAD USING OVERWRITE KEYWORD

```
hive> load data local inpath '/home/cloudera/emp.csv'
    overwrite into table emp;
hive> select * from emp;
```

```
OUTPUT:
1001    hari     d1    chennai    1986-12-10
1002    teja     d1    hyd        1987-01-21
1003    ram      d3    delhi      1986-02-11
1004    milind   d4    bang       1988-03-21
1005    jay      d2    bang       1988-03-22
1006    naveen   d4    hyd        1986-04-12
1007    naser    d1    hyd        1989-11-15
1008    rahul    d3    delhi      1990-12-23
1009    jay      d6    hyd        1988-07-19
```

Verifying through browser after loading from local filesystem using overwrite keyword

Contents of directory /user/hive/warehouse/test.db/emp

Goto : /user/hive/warehouse/test.d [go]

Go to parent directory

Name	Type	Size	Replication	Block Size	Modification Time	Permission	Owner	Group
emp.csv	file	266 B	3	128 MB	2019-06-01 04:22	rw-rw-rw-	cloudera	supergroup

Go back to DFS home

Here, the previous two files emp.csv & emp_copy_1.csv are removed after loading using overwrite keyword. And thereby exists only one emp.csv file

NOTE!!!

- Once the data is loaded to hive table from hadoop filesystem, the file "emp.csv" no more exists in the directory '/user/cloudera/ batch'.

- In other words, loading from hadoop filesystem is like cut and paste to hive; whereas it is like copy & paste when loaded from local filesystem.

- So, if you have already loaded the file (say, emp.csv) from hadoop filesytem, then you can't load or load with overwrite to hive table from hadoop filesystem again....

- And you will get the ERROR: "Invalid path "/user/ cloudera/batch/emp.csv'': No files matching path hdfs://localhost.localdomain:8020/user/ cloudera/batch/emp.csv" because the file is already cut from that location."

Creating & Loading The Department Table

After creating the table again, you can use any of the load method I,e. load from local FS or HDFS with or without overwrite operator

```
hive> create table department(did string,dname
    string,block string) comment 'this is department
    table' row format delimited fields terminated by
    '|' lines terminated by '\n' stored as textfile;

hive> load data local inpath '/home/cloudera/dept.
    csv' overwrite into table department;
hive> select * from department;
```

```
OUTPUT:
d1   research      A-block
d2   sales         A-block
d3   testing       B-block
d4   development   C-block
d5   HR            A-block
```

Verifying the department table through browser

Contents of directory /user/hive/warehouse/test.db/department

Goto : |/user/hive/warehouse/test.d| go

Go to parent directory

Name	Type	Size	Replication	Block Size	Modification Time	Permission	Owner	Group
dept.csv	file	94 B	3	128 MB	2019-06-01 05:04	rw-rw-rw-	cloudera	supergroup

Go back to DFS home

8.5 BASIC OPERATORS, GROUP BY, HAVING, ORDER BY CLAUSES

BUILT_IN RELATIONAL OPERATORS

A=B, A<B, A<=B, A>B, A>=B, A IS NULL, A IS NOT NULL, A LIKE B, A!=B

BUILT_IN ARTHEMATIC OPERATORS

A+B, A-B, A*B, A/B, A%B, A&B, A|B, A^B, ~A
A&B: bitwise and operation
A|B: bitwise or operation
A^B; bitwise XOR operation
~A: bitwise not operation

BUILT_IN LOGICAL OPERATORS

A AND B, A OR B, NOT A

EXERCISE BASED ON BASIC OPERATORS

Q) Display details of employee whose employee id is greater than and equal to 1003 and doesn't come from hyd.

```
hive>select* from emp where id >=1003 and
     place!='hyd';                                        (OR)
hive>select* from emp where id >=1003 and place not
     in('hyd');
```

```
OUTPUT:
1003  ram       d3    delhi      1986-02-11
1004  milind    d4    bang       1988-03-21
1005  jay       d2    bang       1988-03-22
1008  rahul     d3    delhi      1990-12-23
```

Q) Display details of department whose id is less than d2 or department name is development.

```
hive> select * from department where did<'d2' or
   dname='development';
```
(OR)
```
hive> select * from department where did<'d2' or
   dname like 'development';
```
(OR)
```
hive> select * from department where did<'d2' or
   dname like 'd%';
```

```
OUTPUT:
d1 research      A-block
d4 development   C-block
```

Q) Display details of department whose department name's second letter is 'e'.

```
hive> select * from department where did<'d2' or
   dname like '_e%';
```

```
OUTPUT:
d1 research      A-block
d3 testing       B-block
d4 development   C-block
```

Q) Display total no:of employees, minimum of their employee number, avg of their employee number, max of their employee number, sum of their employee number from employee dataset.

```
hive> select count(*),min(id),avg(id),max(id),
   sum(id) from emp;
```

```
OUTPUT:
9   1001    1005.0   1009    9045
```

Q) Display department name, count of employees in each department

```
hive> select count(*),dept from emp group by dept;
```

```
OUTPUT:
3   d1
1   d2
2   d3
2   d4
1   d6
```

Q) Display department name, count of employees in each department and display rows those have count more than 2.

```
hive> select count(*),dept from emp group by dept
        having count(*)>2;
```

```
OUTPUT:
3   d1
```

Q) Display department name, count of employees in each department in descending order of count.

```
hive> select count(*) as c,dept from emp group by
        dept order by c desc;
```

```
OUTPUT:
3   d1
2   d3
2   d4
1   d2
1   d6
```

NOTE!!!
When aggregate functions are used in order by clause then give alias name to aggregte functions as shown above.

Q) Display department name, count of employees in each department in descending order of count and display only first two rows.

```
hive> select count(*) as c,dept from emp group by
      dept order by c desc limit 2;
```

```
OUTPUT:
3   d1
2   d3
```

8.6 JOIN OPERATION AND VIEW

JOIN is a clause that is used for combining specific fields from two tables by using values common to each one. It is used to combine records from two or more tables in the database. A JOIN condition is to be raised using the primary keys and foreign keys of the tables.

There are different types of joins given as follows:

- Join
- Left Outer Join
- Right Outer Join
- Full Outer Join

Simple JOIN

Q) Display the details of employee along with their corresponding department information.

```
hive>select * from emp e join department d on
      (e.dept=d.did);
```

```
OUTPUT:
1001 hari   d1 chennai 1986-12-10 d1 research    A-block
1002 teja   d1 hyd     1987-01-21 d1 research    A-block
1007 naser  d1 hyd     1989-11-15 d1 research    A-block
1005 jay    d2 bang    1988-03-22 d2 sales       A-block
1003 ram    d3 delhi   1986-02-11 d3 testing     B-block
1008 rahul  d3 delhi   1990-12-23 d3 testing     B-block
1004 milind d4 bang    1988-03-21 d4 development C-block
1006 naveen d4 hyd     1986-04-12 d4 development C-block
```

Q) Display the employee no, employee name and corresponding department name those who work in 'A-block'.

```
hive> select id,name,dname from emp e join
    department d on (e.dept=d.did) where d.block='A-
    block';
```

```
OUTPUT:
1001 hari   research
1002 teja   research
1007 naser  research
1005 jay    sales
```

Q) Display the employee name, place, date of birth, department name and its location for the employees whose birthday come in the month of March and are currently working in 'sales' department.

```
hive> select name, place, dob, dname, block from
    emp e join department d on (e.dept=d.did) where
    dob like '%-03-%' and dname='sales';
```

```
OUTPUT:
jay   bang 1988-03-22 sales A-block
```

Left Outer JOIN

A LEFT JOIN returns all the values from the left table, plus the matched values from the right table, or NULL in case of no matching JOIN predicate.

Q) Display details of all the employees in the company along with their current corresponding department details.

```
hive> select * from emp e left outer join department
    d on (e.dept=d.did);
```

```
OUTPUT:
1001 hari    d1 chennai 1986-12-10 d1 research    A-block
1002 teja    d1 hyd     1987-01-21 d1 research    A-block
1007 naser   d1 hyd     1989-11-15 d1 research    A-block
1005 jay     d2 bang    1988-03-22 d2 sales       A-block
1003 ram     d3 delhi   1986-02-11 d3 testing     B-block
1008 rahul   d3 delhi   1990-12-23 d3 testing     B-block
1004 milind  d4 bang    1988-03-21 d4 development C-block
1006 naveen  d4 hyd     1986-04-12 d4 development C-block
1009 jay     d6 hyd     1988-07-19 NULL    NULL       NULL
```

Here employee no 1006 is allocated to a temporary department no 'd6' but the details of that department is not available. Hence, left outer join shows the employee no 1006's other details but corresponding department details are NULL.

Right Outer JOIN

A RIGHT JOIN returns all the values from the right table, plus the matched values from the left table, or NULL in case of no matching join predicate.

Q) Display all the existing department details with their corresponding employee information.

```
hive> select * from emp e right outer join
    department d on (e.dept=d.did);
```

```
OUTPUT:
1001 hari    d1 chennai 1986-12-10 d1 research    A-block
1002 teja    d1 hyd     1987-01-21 d1 research    A-block
1007 naser   d1 hyd     1989-11-15 d1 research    A-block
1005 jay     d2 bang    1988-03-22 d2 sales       A-block
1003 ram     d3 delhi   1986-02-11 d3 testing     B-block
1008 rahul   d3 delhi   1990-12-23 d3 testing     B-block
1004 milind  d4 bang    1988-03-21 d4 development C-block
1006 naveen  d4 hyd     1986-04-12 d4 development C-block
NULL NULL NULL NULL        NULL     d5  HR         A-block
```

Here department no 'd5' is existing in the department table but there are no employees allocated to this department in current scenario and hence, the corresponding employee details are NULL.

Full Outer JOIN

The HiveQL FULL OUTER JOIN combines the records of both the left and the right outer tables that fulfil the JOIN condition. The joined table contains either all the records from both the tables, or fills in NULL values for missing matches on either side.

```
hive> select * from emp e full outer join
    department d on (e.dept=d.did);
```

```
OUTPUT:
1001 hari   d1 chennai 1986-12-10 d1 research    A-block
1002 teja   d1 hyd     1987-01-21 d1 research    A-block
1007 naser  d1 hyd     1989-11-15 d1 research    A-block
1005 jay    d2 bang    1988-03-22 d2 sales       A-block
1003 ram    d3 delhi   1986-02-11 d3 testing     B-block
1008 rahul  d3 delhi   1990-12-23 d3 testing     B-block
1004 milind d4 bang    1988-03-21 d4 development C-block
1006 naveen d4 hyd     1986-04-12 d4 development C-block
NULL NULL   NULL NULL     NULL      d5 HR         A-block
1009 jay    d6 hyd     1988-07-19 NULL  NULL      NULL
```

VIEWS

Apache Hive View is a searchable object in a database which we can define the query. However, we can not store data in the view. View is referred as "virtual tables". Hence, we can query a view like we query on a table. Moreover, by using joins it is possible to combine data from or more table. Also, it contains a subset of information.

To Create a View

Example:
```
hive> create view emp_v as select id,name from emp
    where id>1003;
hive> select * from emp_v;
```

```
OUTPUT:
1004  milind
1005  jay
1006  naveen
1007  naser
1008  rahul
```

To Drop the View

```
hive>drop view emp_v;
```

8.7 BUILT-IN FUNCTIONS

Assume the following file staff.csv in local filesystem

```
$ gedit staff.csv
```

```
1001|hari|d1|chennai|1986-12-10 12:30:56|3.5
1002|teja|d1|hyd|1987-01-21 10:22:40|4
1003|ram|d3|delhi|1986-02-11 10:12:45|9.3
1004|milind|d4|bang|1988-03-21 02:30:55|8.7
1005|jay|d2|bang|1988-03-22 11:30:33|7.5
1006|naveen|d4|hyd|1986-04-12 12:30:33|6.6
1007|naser|d1|hyd|1989-11-15 09:20:50|4.4
1008|rahul|d3|delhi|1990-12-23 10:20:20|10
1009|jay|d6|hyd|1988-07-19 08:45:44|11
```

Create the staff table in Hive and load the above file from local filesystem to Hive

```
Hive> create table staff(id int,name string,dept
   string,place string,dob timestamp,experience
   float) comment 'this  is staff table' row
   format delimited fields terminated by '|' lines
   terminated by '\n' stored as textfile;

hive> load data local inpath '/home/cloudera/staff.
   csv' into table staff;
hive> desc staff;
```

```
OUTPUT:
id          int
name        string
dept        string
place       string
dob         timestamp
experience  float
```

hive> select * from staff;

```
OUTPUT:
1001  hari    d1 chennai  1986-12-10 12:30:56  3.5
1002  teja    d1 hyd      1987-01-21 10:22:40  4.0
1003  ram     d3 delhi    1986-02-11 10:12:45  9.3
1004  milind  d4 bang     1988-03-21 02:30:55  8.7
1005  jay     d2 bang     1988-03-22 11:30:33  7.5
1006  naveen  d4 hyd      1986-04-12 12:30:33  6.6
1007  naser   d1 hyd      1989-11-15 09:20:50  4.4
1008  rahul   d3 delhi    1990-12-23 10:20:20  10.0
1009  jay     d6 hyd      1988-07-19 08:45:44  11.0
```

8.7.1 Round(), Floor(), Ceil()

Example:

hive> select experience, round(experience),
    floor(experience), ceil(experience) from staff;

```
OUTPUT:
3.5    4.0    3     4
4.0    4.0    4     4
9.3    9.0    9     10
8.7    9.0    8     9
7.5    8.0    7     8
6.6    7.0    6     7
4.4    4.0    4     5
10.0   10.0   10    10
11.0   11.0   11    11
```

8.7.2 Date Functions

To_date(): It returns the date part of a timestamp string

```
hive> select to_date(dob) from staff;
```

```
OUTPUT:
1986-12-10
1987-01-21
1986-02-11
1988-03-21
1988-03-22
1986-04-12
1989-11-15
1990-12-23
1988-07-19
```

Year(): It returns the year part of a date or a timestamp string

```
hive> select year(dob) from staff;
```

```
OUTPUT:
1986
1987
1986
1988
1988
1986
1989
1990
1988
```

Month(): It returns the month part of a date or a timestamp string

```
hive> select month(dob) from staff;
```

```
OUTPUT:
12
1
2
3
3
4
11
12
7
```

Day(): It returns the day part of a date or a timestamp string

```
hive> select day(dob) from staff;
```

```
OUTPUT:
10
21
11
21
22
12
15
23
19
```

Q) Display staff id, name, years of experience and date of birth whose birthday falls in the month of December having experience is in range 3–10 years.

```
hive> select id, name, dob, experience from staff
    where month(dob)=12 and (experience between
    3 and 10);
```

```
OUTPUT:
1001  hari  1986-12-10 12:30:56   3.5
1008  rahul 1990-12-23 10:20:20   10.0
```

8.7.3 String Functions

CAST(): It converts the results of the expression expr to <type>. A NULL is returned if the conversion does not succeed.

```
hive> select cast(experience as double) from staff;
```

```
OUTPUT:
3.5
4.0
9.300000190734863
8.699999809265137
7.5
6.599999904632568
4.400000095367432
10.0
11.0
```

> **NOTE!!**
> String position starts from index '1' and not from '0'

substr (string A, int start): It returns the substring of A starting from start position till the end of string A.

```
hive> select (name),substr(name,2) from staff;
```

```
OUTPUT:
hari      ari
teja      eja
ram       am
milind    ilind
jay       ay
naveen    aveen
naser     aser
rahul     ahul
jay       ay
```

substr (string A, int start, int length): It returns the substring of A starting from start position with the given length.

```
hive> select (name),substr(name,1,2) from staff;
```

```
OUTPUT:
hari        ha
teja        te
ram         ra
milind      mi
jay         ja
naveen      na
naser       na
rahul       ra
jay         ja
```

```
hive> select substr(name,1,3) from emp;
```

```
OUTPUT:
har
tej
ram
mil
jay
nav
nas
rah
jay
```

```
hive> select substr(name,3,2) from emp;
```

```
OUTPUT:
ri
ja
m
li
y
ve
se
hu
y
```

concat (string A, string B,...): It returns the string resulting from concatenating B after A.

```
hive> select concat(name,experience) from staff;
```

OUTPUT:
```
hari3.5
teja4.0
ram9.3
milind8.7
jay7.5
naveen6.6
naser4.4
rahul10.0
jay11.0
```

upper (string A) or ucase (string A): It returns the string resulting from converting all characters of A to upper case.

```
hive> select (name),ucase(name) from staff;        (OR)
hive> select (name),upper(name) from staff;
```

OUTPUT:
```
hari        HARI
teja        TEJA
ram         RAM
milind      MILIND
jay         JAY
naveen      NAVEEN
naser       NASER
rahul       RAHUL
jay         JAY
```

lower (string A) or lcase (string A): It returns the string resulting from converting all characters of B to lower case.

```
hive> select (name),lcase(name) from staff;        (OR)
hive> select (name),lower(name) from staff;
```

OUTPUT:
```
hari        hari
teja        teja
ram         ram
milind      milind
jay         jay
```

```
naveen      naveen
naser       naser
rahul       rahul
jay         jay
```

regexp_replace (string A, string B, string C): It returns the string resulting from replacing all substrings in A by string C that matches the Java regular expression syntax with string B.

Q) Display the places of staffs after replacing old name 'bang' to 'bengaluru'.

```
hive> select (place),regexp_replace(place,'bang',
     'bengaluru') from staff;
```

```
OUTPUT:
chennai     chennai
hyd         hyd
delhi       delhi
bang        bengaluru
babng       bengaluru
hyd         hyd
hyd         hyd
delhi       delhi
hyd         hyd
```

Exercise:

1. trim (string A): It returns the string resulting from trimming spaces from both ends of A.

2. ltrim (string A): It returns the string resulting from trimming spaces from the beginning (left hand side) of A.

3. rtrim (string A): rtrim (string A) It returns the string resulting from trimming spaces from the end (right hand side) of A.

8.8 STORE THE OUTPUT OF ANALYSIS

8.8.1 To Store the Output of Analysis to Some Other Table

Example 1:

Step 1: Create a new table with schema similar to the output to be generated.

```
create table abc(num string,ename string,place
   string);
```

Step 2: Store the output of analysis to the newly created table.

```
hive> insert overwrite table abc select id,name,
   place from emp where id>1003 and place not
   in ('chennai');
hive> select * from abc;
```

```
OUTPUT:
1004    milind    bang
1005    jay       bang
1006    naveen    hyd
1007    naser     hyd
1008    rahul     delhi
1009    jay       hyd
```

Example 2:

Step 1: Create a new table with schema similar to the output to be generated.

```
hive> create table abc as select * from emp;
hive> select * from abc;
```

Step 2: Store the output of analysis to the newly created table.

```
hive> insert overwrite table abc select * from emp
   where id>1003;
hive> select * from abc;
```

```
OUTPUT:
1004   milind   d4   bang    1988-03-21
1005   jay      d2   bang    1988-03-22
1006   naveen   d4   hyd     1986-04-12
1007   naser    d1   hyd     1989-11-15
1008   rahul    d3   delhi   1990-12-23
1009   jay      d6   hyd     1988-07-19
```

8.8.2 To Store the Output of Analysis to HDFS

```
hive> insert overwrite directory '/user/cloudera/
   output1'  select * from emp where id>1003;
```

Note!!

Here, output1 is a new directory in /user/cloudera, which will be created automatically.

To verify the output file in Hadoop file system

```
$ hadoop fs -ls /user/cloudera/output1
$ hadoop fs -cat /user/cloudera/output1/00000_0
```
(or)
```
hive> dfs -ls /user/cloudera/output1;
```

```
-rw-r--r-- 3 cloudera supergroup 149 2018-04-17
   03:32 /user/cloudera/output1/000000_0
```

```
hive> dfs -cat /user/cloudera/output1/0*;
```

```
OUTPUT:
1004milindd4bang1988-03-21
1005jayd2bang1988-03-22
1006naveend4hyd1986-04-12
1007naserd1hyd1989-11-15
1008rahuld3delhi1990-12-23
```

(or)

To verify through browser

File: /user/cloudera/output1/000000_0

Goto : |/user/cloudera/output1 | [go]

Go back to dir listing
Advanced view/download options

```
1004milindd4bang1988-03-21
1005jayd2bang1988-03-22
1006naveend4hyd1986-04-12
1007naserd1hyd1989-11-15
1008rahuld3delhi1990-12-23
```

8.8.3 To Store The Output Of Analysis To Local File System

```
hive> insert overwrite local directory '/home/
   cloudera/output1' select * from employee where
   id>1003;
```

To verify the output in local file system

```
$ ls
$ cd output1
$ cat 000000_0    (OR)  $ gedit 000000_0
```

(OR)

```
$ ls output1
$ cat output1/000000_0
```

TO QUIT FROM HIVE

```
hive> quit;
```

8.9 MANAGED V/S EXTERNAL TABLE

Managed and External tables are the two different types of tables in hive used to improve how data is loaded, managed and controlled.

Managed Table

- Managed table is also called as Internal table. This is the default table in Hive. When we create a table in Hive without specifying it as external, by default we will get a Managed table.

- If we create a table as a managed table, the table will be created in a specific location in HDFS.

- By default, the table data will be created in /usr/hive/warehouse directory of HDFS.

- If we delete a Managed table, both the table data and meta data for that table will be deleted from the HDFS.

Assume the following file staff.csv in local filesystem

```
$ gedit staff.csv
1001|hari|d1|chennai|1986-12-10 12:30:56|3.5
1002|teja|d1|hyd|1987-01-21 10:22:40|4
1003|ram|d3|delhi|1986-02-11 10:12:45|9.3
1004|milind|d4|bang|1988-03-21 02:30:55|8.7
1005|jay|d2|bang|1988-03-22 11:30:33|7.5
1006|naveen|d4|hyd|1986-04-12 12:30:33|6.6
1007|naser|d1|hyd|1989-11-15 09:20:50|4.4
1008|rahul|d3|delhi|1990-12-23 10:20:20|10
1009|jay|d6|hyd|1988-07-19 08:45:44|11
```

Step 1: Create Managed table as follow:

```
hive> create table staff(id int,name string,dept
    string,place string,dob timestamp,experience
    float) row format delimited fields terminated by
    '|' lines terminated by '\n' stored as textfile;
```

After successfully creating the table, check the details of the table type as shown in the below command:

```
hive> describe formatted staff;
```

```
# col_name              data_type              comment

id                      int                    None
name                    string                 None
dept                    string                 None
place                   string                 None
dob                     timestamp              None
experience              float                  None

# Detailed Table Information
Database:               test
Owner:                  cloudera
CreateTime:             Mon Jun 03 04:13:06 PDT 2019
LastAccessTime:         UNKNOWN
Protect Mode:           None
Retention:              0
Location:               hdfs://localhost.localdomain:8020/user/hive/warehouse/test.db/staff
Table Type:             MANAGED_TABLE
Table Parameters:
        transient_lastDdlTime    1559560386

# Storage Information
SerDe Library:          org.apache.hadoop.hive.serde2.lazy.LazySimpleSerDe
InputFormat:            org.apache.hadoop.mapred.TextInputFormat
OutputFormat:           org.apache.hadoop.hive.ql.io.HiveIgnoreKeyTextOutputFormat
Compressed:             No
Num Buckets:            -1
Bucket Columns:         []
Sort Columns:           []
Storage Desc Params:
        field.delim          |
        line.delim           \n
        serialization.format |
Time taken: 1.007 seconds
```

In the above image we can see **MANAGED_TABLE as the entry for the option Table type** which means that we have created a Managed table.

Step 2: Now, we will load one sample dataset into the table by using the below command:

```
hive> load data local inpath '/home/cloudera/staff.
   csv' into table staff;
hive> select * from staff;
```

```
OUTPUT:
1001  hari     d1  chennai  1986-12-10  12:30:56  3.5
1002  teja     d1  hyd      1987-01-21  10:22:40  4.0
1003  ram      d3  delhi    1986-02-11  10:12:45  9.3
1004  milind   d4  bang     1988-03-21  02:30:55  8.7
1005  jay      d2  bang     1988-03-22  11:30:33  7.5
1006  naveen   d4  hyd      1986-04-12  12:30:33  6.6
1007  naser    d1  hyd      1989-11-15  09:20:50  4.4
1008  rahul    d3  delhi    1990-12-23  10:20:20  10.0
1009  jay      d6  hyd      1988-07-19  08:45:44  11.0
```

Step 3: Check the contents of the table in HDFS by using the below command:

```
$ hadoop fs -ls hdfs://localhost:/user/hive/
    warehouse/test.db/staff
```

```
-rw-rw-rw-    3 cloudera supergroup       378
    2019-06-03 04:21
    hdfs://localhost:/user/hive/warehouse/test.db/
    staff/staff.csv
```

Step 4: Now drop the table using the below command:

```
hive> drop table staff;
```

```
OK
Time taken: 0.604 seconds
```

Step 5: Now, try to check the contents of the table in HDFS using the below command again:

```
$ hadoop fs -ls hdfs://localhost:/user/hive/
    warehouse/test.db/staff
```

```
ls: 'hdfs://localhost:/user/hive/warehouse/test.
    db/staff': No such file or directory
```

In the above image, you can see that it is displaying like **No such file or directory** because both the table and its contents are deleted from the HDFS location.

External Table

External table is created for external use as when the data is used outside Hive. Whenever we want to delete the table's meta data and we want to keep the table's data as it is, we use External table. External table only deletes the schema of the table.

Step 1: Let us create an external table by using the below command:

```
$ create external table staff(id int,name string,dept
    string,place string,dob timestamp,experience
    float) row format delimited fields terminated by
    '|' lines terminated by '\n' stored as textfile;
```

After successfully creating the table, check the details of the table type as shown in the below command:

```
hive> describe formatted staff;
```

```
# col_name              data_type            comment

id                      int                  None
name                    string               None
dept                    string               None
place                   string               None
dob                     timestamp            None
experience              float                None

# Detailed Table Information
Database:               test
Owner:                  cloudera
CreateTime:             Mon Jun 03 04:37:08 PDT 2019
LastAccessTime:         UNKNOWN
Protect Mode:           None
Retention:              0
Location:               hdfs://localhost.localdomain:8020/user/hive/warehouse/test.db/staff
Table Type:             EXTERNAL_TABLE
Table Parameters:
        EXTERNAL              TRUE
        transient_lastDdlTime 1559561828

# Storage Information
SerDe Library:          org.apache.hadoop.hive.serde2.lazy.LazySimpleSerDe
InputFormat:            org.apache.hadoop.mapred.TextInputFormat
OutputFormat:           org.apache.hadoop.hive.ql.io.HiveIgnoreKeyTextOutputFormat
Compressed:             No
Num Buckets:            -1
Bucket Columns:         []
Sort Columns:           []
Storage Desc Params:
        field.delim          |
        line.delim           \n
        serialization.format |
Time taken: 0.292 seconds
```

In the above image we can see the **EXTERNAL_TABLE as the entry for the option Table type** which says that the above table is an External table.

Step 2: Now let us load some data into the table using the below command:

```
hive> load data local inpath '/home/cloudera/staff.
   csv' into table staff;
hive> select * from staff;
```

```
OUTPUT:
1001  hari    d1  chennai  1986-12-10 12:30:56 3.5
1002  teja    d1  hyd      1987-01-21 10:22:40 4.0
1003  ram     d3  delhi    1986-02-11 10:12:45 9.3
1004  milind  d4  bang     1988-03-21 02:30:55 8.7
1005  jay     d2  bang     1988-03-22 11:30:33 7.5
1006  naveen  d4  hyd      1986-04-12 12:30:33 6.6
```

```
1007  naser    d1  hyd      1989-11-15 09:20:50 4.4
1008  rahul    d3  delhi    1990-12-23 10:20:20 10.0
1009  jay      d6  hyd      1988-07-19 08:45:44 11.0
```

Step 3: Check the contents of the table in HDFS by using the below command:

```
$ hadoop fs -ls hdfs://localhost:/user/hive/
   warehouse/test.db/staff
```

```
-rw-rw-rw-    3 cloudera supergroup           378
   2019-06-03 04:41
   hdfs://localhost:/user/hive/warehouse/test.db/
   staff/staff.csv
```

Step 4: Now drop the table using the below command:

```
hive> drop table staff;
```

```
OK
Time taken: 0.604 seconds
```

Step 5: Now, try to check the contents of the table in HDFS using the below command again:

```
$ hadoop fs -ls hdfs://localhost:/user/hive/
   warehouse/test.db/staff
```

```
-rw-rw-rw-    3 cloudera supergroup           378
   2019-06-03 04:41
   hdfs://localhost:/user/hive/warehouse/test.db/
   staff/staff.csv
```

Here, we can see that the contents of the table are still present in the HDFS location. If we create an External table, after deleting the table only the meta data related to table is deleted but not the contents of the table. This approach works only if the data is in **/user/hive/warehouse (default)** directory.

Step 6: Let us create external table in another location in HDFS other than default location (**/user/hive/warehouse** directory). In this case if we delete the table, the data will also get deleted. So, here we need to mention the **external location** of the data while creating the table itself as shown below.

Step 6.1: Create external table in new path '/user/cloudera/testex'. Create 'testex' directory before running the below command using the argument '-mkdir'

```
hive> create table staff(id int,name string,dept
    string,place string,dob timestamp,experience
    float) row format delimited fields terminated by
    '|' lines terminated by '\n' stored as textfile
    location '/user/cloudera/testex';
```

To Verify whether a directory is created for the above external table

```
$ hadoop fs -ls /user/cloudera/
```

```
drwxr-xr-x    - cloudera cloudera 0 2019-06-03 23:48
    /user/cloudera/testex
```

Step 6.2: Load the data from local filesystem to newly created external table.

```
hive> load data local inpath '/home/cloudera/staff.
    csv' into table staff;
```

To verify the file loaded to HDFS

Contents of directory /user/cloudera/testex

Goto : /user/cloudera/testex   go

Go to parent directory

Name	Type	Size	Replication	Block Size	Modification Time	Permission	Owner	Group
staff.csv	file	378 B	3	128 MB	2019-06-03 23:49	rw-r--r--	cloudera	cloudera

Go back to DFS home

Step 6.3 Drop the external table

```
hive> drop table staff;
OK
Time taken: 0.113 seconds
```

To verify the presence of data in external table after drop command

```
$ hadoop fs -ls /user/cloudera/testex/
ls: '/user/cloudera/testex/': No such file or directory
```

8.10 DATA TYPES

Hive supports different types of data types both primitive and complex data types.

Primitive data types are:

Numeric Types

- **TINYINT:** 1-byte signed integer, from -128 to 127
- **SMALLINT:** 2-byte signed integer, from -32,768 to 32,767
- **INT:** 4-byte signed integer, from -2,147,483,648 to 2,147,483,647
- **BIGINT:** 8-byte signed integer, from -9,223,372,036,854,775,808 to 9,223,372,036,854,775,807
- **FLOAT:** 4-byte single precision floating point number
- **DOUBLE:** 8-byte double precision floating point number
- **DECIMAL:** Hive 0.13.0 introduced user definable precision and scale

String Types

- STRING
- VARCHAR
- CHAR

Date/Time Types

- TIMESTAMP
- DATE

Misc Types

- BOOLEAN
- BINARY

Apart from these primitive data types, Hive offers some complex data types like:

Complex Data Types

- **arrays**: ARRAY<data_type>

- **maps**: MAP<primitive_type, data_type>

- **structs**: STRUCT<col_name: data_type [COMMENT col_comment], ...>

EXERCISE ON COMPLEX DATA TYPES:

8.10.1 Arrays

It is a collection of items of similar data type. i.e, it contains one or more values of the same data type.

Let us take an example of student dataset from secondary school where the fields are delimited by tab and the complex data type Array values are delimited by the comma.

```
$ gedit student.txt
1001    Hari    55,70,65,74,82
1002    Teja    70,49,68,77,50
1003    Lata    66,70,56,70,65
1004    Lalit   90,78,86,71,85
1005    Neha    85,79,80,75,69
```

Here, the fields represent student no, name, five subject marks{physics, chemistry, Math, science, English} respectively.

Let us create a table to store the above values of student dataset using below code.

```
hive> create table student(sno int,name
    string,marks array<int>) row format delimited
    fields terminated by '\t' collection items
    terminated by ',' lines terminated by '\n' stored
    as textfile;
```

Load the above table with student.txt dataset stored in local file system

```
hive> load data local inpath '/home/cloudera/
    student.txt' into table student;
```

To View the content of the table

```
hive> select * from student;
```

```
1001    Hari    [55,70,65,74,82]
1002    Teja    [70,49,68,77,50]
1003    Lata    [66,70,56,70,65]
1004    Lalit   [90,78,86,71,85]
1005    Neha    [85,79,80,75,69]
Time taken: 1.532 seconds
```

To See the schema of the table

```
hive> describe student;
```

```
sno        int
name       string
marks      array<int>
```

Q) Display the student name along with their corresponding Math subject marks.

```
hive> select name,marks[2] from student;
```

```
OUTPUT:
Hari       65
Teja       68
Lata       56
Lalit      86
Neha       80
```

Q) Display the highest mark in English and physics among the students.

```
hive> select max(marks[4]) as highest_english,
    max(marks[0]) as highest_physics from student ;
```

```
OUTPUT:
85 90
```

8.10.2 Map

Map is a collection of key-value pairs where fields are accessed using array notation of keys. For e.g: ['Key']

In our Map example we will be using the dataset population.txt where the fields are delimited by tab, the complex type Map values are delimited by the comma.

```
$ gedit population.txt
Delhi    male    2015:2566,2016:3045,2017:3000,2018:2430
Delhi    female  2015:4350,2016:1880,2017:2550,2018:3450
Goa      male    2015:1033,2016:506,2017:890,2018:730
Goa      female  2015:970,2016:345,2017:560,2018:550
Kerala   male    2015:650,2016:1330,2017:1055,2018:1432
Kerala   female  2015:980,2016:1260,2017:1160,2018:2345
Orissa   male    2015:1230,2016:2450,2017:2690,2018:3475
Orissa   female  2015:2440,2016:1680,2017:2550,2018:1650
```

Here, Map field value represents no: of male or female children born in a particular month of a year.

Let us create a table to store the above values of population dataset using below code.

```
hive> create table pop(place string,gender string,
    cnt map<int,int>) row format delimited fields
    terminated by '\t' collection items terminated by
    ',' map keys terminated by ':';
```

NOTE!! In the create table syntax, the commands like lines terminated by '\n'
stored as textfile are optional because by default lines are terminated by '\n' and the files are stored as text files.

Load the above table with population.txt dataset stored in local file system

```
hive> load data local inpath '/home/cloudera/
    population.txt' into table pop;
```

To View the content of the table

```
hive> select * from pop;
```

```
OUTPUT:
Delhi   male    {2015:2566,2016:3045,2017:3000,2018:2430}
Delhi   female  {2015:4350,2016:1880,2017:2550,2018:3450}
Goa     male    {2015:1033,2016:506,2017:890,2018:730}
Goa     female  {2015:970,2016:345,2017:560,2018:550}
Kerala  male    {2015:650,2016:1330,2017:1055,2018:1432}
Kerala  female  {2015:980,2016:1260,2017:1160,2018:2345}
Orissa  male    {2015:1230,2016:2450,2017:2690,2018:3475}
Orissa  female  {2015:2440,2016:1680,2017:2550,2018:1650}
```

To See the schema of the table

```
hive> describe pop;
```

```
place string
gender      string
cnt map<int,int>
```

Q) Display the count of male and female child born in the year 2017 in 'Delhi'.

```
hive> select cnt[2017] from pop where place='Delhi';
```

```
OUTPUT:
3000
2550
```

Q) Display the place, count of female child according to above dataset in the year 2018 in decreasing order of the count.

```
hive> select place, cnt[2018] as c from pop where
    gender='female' order by c desc;
```

```
OUTPUT:
Delhi     3450
Kerala    2345
Orissa    1650
Goa       550
```

8.10.3 Struct

Struct is a record type which encapsulates a set of named fields that can be any primitive data type. An element in STRUCT type can be accessed using the DOT (.) notation.

In our Struct example, we will be using the dataset class.txt where the fields are delimited by tab and the complex type Array values are delimited by the comma.

```
$ gedit class.txt
S001  Mayank,8.7,5,CSE
S101  teja,8,6,ISE
S002  Milind,6.8,6,CSE
S104  Hima,9.4,5,ISE
S008  Naidu,9.5,6,CSE
S110  Nayan,7.3,5,ISE
```

Here, first field represent student roll no and the second field describes student details like name, CGPA, Semester, department.

Let us create a table to store the above values of student dataset using below code.

```
hive> create table StudentDetail(sno string,
    Sdetail struct<name:string,CGPA:float,
    sem:int,dept:string>) row format delimited
    fields terminated by '\t' collection items
    terminated by ',';
```

Load the above table with class.txt dataset stored in local file system

```
hive> load data local inpath '/home/cloudera/class.
    txt' into table StudentDetail;
```

To View the content of the table

```
hive> select * from StudentDetail;
```

```
OUTPUT:
S001  {"name":"Mayank","cgpa":8.7,"sem":5,"dept":"CSE"}
S101  {"name":"teja","cgpa":8.0,"sem":6,"dept":"ISE"}
S002  {"name":"Milind","cgpa":6.8,"sem":6,"dept":"CSE"}
```

```
S104   {"name":"Hima","cgpa":9.4,"sem":5,"dept":"ISE"}
S008   {"name":"Naidu","cgpa":9.5,"sem":6,"dept":"CSE"}
S110   {"name":"Nayan","cgpa":7.3,"sem":5,"dept":"ISE"}
```

To See the schema of the table

```
hive> describe StudentDetail;
sno        string
sdetail    struct<name:string,CGPA:float,
    sem:int,dept:string>
```

Q) Display all the student name from the above dataset.

```
hive> select sdetail.name from StudentDetail;
```

```
OUTPUT:
Mayank
teja
Milind
Hima
Naidu
Nayan
```

Q) Display the student roll no, name of 5th semester students.

```
hive> select sno,sdetail.name from StudentDetail
    where sdetail.sem=5;
```

```
OUTPUT:
S001  Mayank
S104  Hima
S110  Nayan
```

Q) Display student name, CGPA, Department name of CSE students in decreasing order of their CGPA.

```
hive> select sdetail.name,sdetail.CGPA as cgpa,
    sdetail.dept from StudentDetail where sdetail.
    dept='CSE' order by cgpa;
```

```
OUTPUT:
Naidu       9.5    CSE
Mayank      8.7    CSE
Milind      6.8    CSE
```

Chapter 9

HBase

9.1 INTRODUCTION

- HBase is a distributed **column-oriented database** built on top of the Hadoop file system.

- It is an open-source project and is horizontally scalable.

- HBase is a data model that is similar to Google's big table designed to provide quick random access to huge amounts of structured data.

- One can store the data in HDFS either directly or through HBase.

- Data consumer reads/accesses the data in HDFS randomly using HBase.

- HBase sits on top of the Hadoop File System and provides read and write access.

Hbase and HDFS

HDFS	HBase
HDFS is a distributed file system suitable for storing large files.	HBase is a database built on top of the HDFS.
HDFS does not support fast individual record lookups.	HBase provides fast lookups for larger tables.
It provides high latency batch processing; no concept of batch processing.	It provides low latency access to single rows from billions of records (Random access).
It provides only sequential access of data.	HBase internally uses Hash tables and provides random access, and it stores the data in indexed HDFS files for faster lookups.

Storage Mechanism in HBase

HBase is a **column-oriented database** and the tables in it are sorted by row. The table schema defines only column families, which are the key value pairs.

- Table is a collection of rows.

- Row is a collection of column families.

- Column family is a collection of columns.

- Column is a collection of key value pairs.

Strengths of HBase

- We should use HBase where we have large data sets (millions or billions or rows and columns) and we require fast, random and real time, read and write access over the data.

- The data sets are distributed across various clusters and we need high scalability to handle data.

- The data is gathered from various data sources and it is either semi structured or unstructured data or a combination of all. It could be handled easily with HBase.

- You want to store column-oriented data.

- You have lots of versions of the data sets and you need to store all of them.

9.2 LOGICAL REPRESENTATION OF A TABLE IN HBASE AND VARIOUS COMMANDS

EMPLOYEE TABLE

Row Key	Personal Data		Professional Data	
	Name	City	Designation	Salary
1	Raju	Hyd	Manager	50000
2	Milind	Chennai	Soft engineer	30000
3	Anita	Delhi	Tester	40000

Here, each row is identified by Row key no as 1,2,3. Personal Data and Professional Data are the two column families. The columns Name, city belong to Personal Data and Designation, salary belong to Professional Data

TO START HBASE

```
$ hbase shell
```

GENERAL SHELL COMMANDS

```
hbase(main):001:0> status
1 servers, 0 dead, 2.0000 average load

hbase(main):002:0> version
1.2.0-cdh5.13.0, rUnknown, Wed Oct  4 11:16:18 PDT
   2017

hbase(main):003:0> whoami
cloudera (auth:SIMPLE)
    groups: cloudera, default

hbase(main):004:0> table_help
Help for table-reference commands.
```

9.2.1 Create Table & Store Data

Creating the table and loading the data as shown in above logical representation

```
hbase(main):007:0> create 'emp','personal data',
   'professional data'
hbase(main):008:0> describe 'emp'
```

To Verify table

```
hbase(main):008:0> list
```

```
TABLE
emp
```

```
hbase(main):014:0> exists 'emp'
```

```
Table emp does exist
```

Insertion of data to first row

```
hbase(main):009:0>put 'emp','row1','personal
    data:name','raju'
hbase(main):010:0>put 'emp','row1','personal
    data:city','hyd'
hbase(main):011:0>put 'emp','row1','professional
    data:designation','manager'
hbase(main):012:0>put 'emp','row1','professional
    data:salary','50000'
```

To view the content in the table

```
hbase(main):013:0> scan 'emp'
```

```
ROW                        COLUMN+CELL
row1                       column=personal data:city,
    timestamp=1523425226089, value=hyd
row1                       column=personal data:name,
    timestamp=1523425200247, value=raju
row1                       column=professional
    data:designation, timestamp=1523425255478,
    value=manager
row1                       column=professional
    data:salary, timestamp=1523425270378,
    value=50000
```

Insertion of data to second row

```
hbase(main):013:0> put 'emp','row2','personal
    data:name','milind'
hbase(main):018:0> put 'emp','row2','personal
    data:city','chennai'
hbase(main):020:0> put 'emp','row2','professional
    data:designation','soft Engineer'
hbase(main):015:0> put 'emp','row2','professional
    data:salary','30000'
```

Insertion of data to third row

```
hbase(main):022:0> put 'emp','row3','personal
    data:name','anita'
hbase(main):023:0> put 'emp','row3','personal
    data:city','delhi'
hbase(main):024:0> put 'emp','row3','professional
    data:designation','tester'
hbase(main):025:0> put 'emp','row3','professional
    data:salary','40000'
```

9.2.2 Read the Data Row-wise and Cell-wise

SCAN: It is used to read all rows of a table

Q) Display all the details of employees.

```
hbase(main):026:0> scan 'emp'
```

```
ROW                      COLUMN+CELL
row1 column=personal data:city,
    timestamp=1523426980414, value=hyd
row1 column=personal data:name,
    timestamp=1523426797711, value=raju
row1 column=professional data:designation,
    timestamp=1523426835511, value=manager
row1 column=professional data:salary,
    timestamp=1523426852045, value=50000
row2 column=personal data:city,
    timestamp=1523427018284, value=chennai
row2 column=personal data:name,
    timestamp=1523426910414, value=milind
row2 column=professional data:designation,
    timestamp=1523427061723, value=soft Engineer
row2 column=professional data:salary,
    timestamp=1523426965356, value=30000
row3 column=personal data:city,
    timestamp=1523427129733, value=delhi
```

```
row3 column=personal data:name,
    timestamp=1523427115249, value=anita
row3 column=professional data:designation,
    timestamp=1523427162000, value=tester
row3 column=professional data:salary,
    timestamp=1523427187838, value=40000
row3(s) in 0.0190 seconds
```

GET: It is used to read data of a particular row or specific column

Q) Display the details of employee named as 'Anita'.

```
hbase(main):027:0> get    'emp','row3'
```

```
COLUMN                              CELL
personal data:city                  timestamp=
    1523427129733, value=delhi
personal data:name                  timestamp=
    1523427115249, value=anita
professional data:designation       timestamp=
    1523427162000, value=tester
professional data:salary            timestamp=
    1523427187838, value=40000
```

Q) Find the city to which Anita belongs?

```
hbase(main):004:0> get
    'emp','row3',{COLUMN=>'personal  data:city'}
```

```
COLUMN                      CELL
personal data:city          timestamp=1523427129733,
                            value=delhi
```

NOTE!!!
COLUMN must be in CAPITAL letters and this keyword is used to get content of a particular cell

9.2.3 To Update/Modify the Existing Data

Q) Update the city of Anita to 'Bangalore', 'Kochi' and later to 'Dehradun' as she changes her city due to work.

```
hbase(main):008:0> put 'emp','row3','personal
    data:city','2bang'
hbase(main):009:0> put 'emp','row3','personal
    data:city','3kochi'
```

To display all the updated values together

```
hbase(main):010:0> get 'emp','row3',{COLUMN=>
    'personal data:city',VERSIONS=>3}
```

```
COLUMN                  CELL
personal data:city      timestamp=1523428351922,
    value=3kochi
personal data:city      timestamp=1523428337355,
    value=2bang
personal data:city      timestamp=1523427129733,
    value=delhi
```

Here, the keyword 'VERSIONS' indicate history or different versions of value that a particular cell has.

To update the 'city' of Anita to 'Dehradun' and Analyze the use of keyword 'VERSIONS'

```
hbase(main):011:0> put 'emp','row3','personal
    data:city','4dehradun'
hbase(main):012:0> get 'emp','row3',{COLUMN=>'personal
    data:city',VERSIONS=>3}
```

```
COLUMN                              CELL
personal data:city      timestamp=1523428391129,
    value=4dehradun
personal data:city      timestamp=1523428351922,
    value=3kochi
personal data:city      timestamp=1523428337355,
    value=2bang
```

Q) Display the latest two cities that Anita has stayed for her official work.

```
hbase(main):013:0> get 'emp','row3',
   {COLUMN=>'personal data:city',VERSIONS=>2}
```

COLUMN	CELL
personal data:city value=4dehradun	timestamp=1523428391129,
personal data:city value=3kochi	timestamp=1523428351922,

9.2.4 Alter Command

Alter command is used to make changes to an existing table. It is used to change the Versions of a column family, set and delete table scope operators, and add or delete a column family from a table.

DISABLE A TABLE

- To delete a table or change its settings, you need to first disable the table using the disable command. You can re-enable it using the enable command.

- AFTER disable: "list" command will display the table name but "scan" command command will show error.

```
hbase(main):024:0> disable 'emp'
hbase(main):020:0> list
```

```
OUTPUT:
TABLE
emp
example
expert
```

```
hbase(main):027:0> scan 'emp'
```

```
OUTPUT:
ROW                        COLUMN+CELL
ERROR: org.apache.hadoop.hbase.DoNotRetry
   IOException: expert is disabled.
```

is_disabled

This command is used to find whether a table is disabled. Its syntax is as follows. If it is disabled, it will return true and if not, it will return false.

```
hbase(main):031:0> is_disabled 'emp'
```

```
true
0 row(s) in 0.0440 seconds
```

disable_all

This command is used to disable all the tables matching the given regular expression.

```
Hbase(main):006:0> disable_all 'ex.*'
```

```
example
exp
expert

Disable the above 3 tables (y/n)?
y
3 tables successfully disabled
```

USING ALTER COMMAND TO ADD ADDITIONAL COLUMN FAMILY 'XYZ' WITH VERSIONS AS '5'

```
hbase(main):017:0> disable 'emp'
hbase(main):018:0> alter 'emp',NAME=>'xyz',
    VERSIONS=>5
hbase(main):020:0> enable 'emp'
```

To see schema of the table after adding one more column family

```
hbase(main):022:0> describe 'emp'
```

```
DESCRIPTION
ENABLED
{NAME => 'personal data', DATA_BLOCK_ENCODING =>
    'NONE', BLOOMFI
 LTER => 'NONE', REPLICATION_SCOPE => '0',
    VERSIONS => '3', COMPRESSION => 'NONE', MIN_
    VERSIONS => '0,
```

```
', TTL => '2147483647', KEEP_DELETED_CELLS =>
'false', BLOCKSIZE => '65536', IN_MEMORY =>
'false', E
NCODE_ON_DISK => 'true', BLOCKCACHE => 'true'},
{NAME => 'professional data', DATA_BLOCK_
ENCODING =>
'NONE', BLOOMFILTER => 'NONE', REPLICATION_SCOPE
=> '0', VERSIONS => '3', COMPRESSION => 'NONE',
MI
N_VERSIONS => '0', TTL => '2147483647', KEEP_
DELETED_CELLS => 'false', BLOCKSIZE => '65536',
IN_MEMO
RY => 'false', ENCODE_ON_DISK => 'true',
BLOCKCACHE => 'true'}, {NAME => 'emp', FAMILIES
=> [{NAME => 'xyz', DATA_BLOCK_ENCODING =>
'NONE', BLOOMFILTER => 'NON true
E', REPLICATION_SCOPE => '0', COMPRESSION =>
'NONE', VERSIONS => '5', TTL => '2147483647',
MIN_VERSI
ONS => '0', KEEP_DELETED_CELLS => 'false',
BLOCKSIZE => '65536', ENCODE_ON_DISK => 'true',
IN_MEMORY
=> 'false', BLOCKCACHE => 'true'},]}
```

To insert data into newly created column family 'xyz'

```
hbase(main):023:0> put
   'emp','row3','xyz:city','5mumbai'
hbase(main):024:0> put
   'emp','row3','xyz:city','6jodhpur'
hbase(main):028:0> put
   'emp','row3','xyz:city','7hubli'
hbase(main):029:0> put
   'emp','row3','xyz:city','8london'
hbase(main):030:0> put
   'emp','row3','xyz:city','9shimla'
hbase(main):031:0> put
   'emp','row3','xyz:city','10kanpur'
hbase(main):032:0> put
   'emp','row3','xyz:city','11nagpur'
```

To read the latest 5 updated value of city column of 'xyz'

```
hbase(main):033:0> get 'emp','row3',
  {COLUMN=>'xyz:city',VERSIONS=>5}
```

```
OUTPUT:
COLUMN                CELL
xyz:city   timestamp=1523431975773, value=11nagpur
xyz:city   timestamp=1523431968306, value=10kanpur
xyz:city   timestamp=1523431961690, value=9shimla
xyz:city   timestamp=1523431953548, value=8london
xyz:city   timestamp=1523431947056, value=7hubli
5 row(s) in 0.0080 seconds
```

To read the entire content of table 'emp'

```
hbase(main):034:0> scan 'emp'
```

```
OUTPUT:
ROW                   COLUMN+CELL
row1 column=personal data:city,
   timestamp=1523426980414, value=hyd
row1 column=personal data:name,
   timestamp=1523426797711, value=raju
row1 column=professional data:designation,
   timestamp=1523426835511, value=manager
row1 column=professional data:salary,
   timestamp=1523426852045, value=50000
row2 column=personal data:city,
   timestamp=1523427018284, value=chennai
row2 column=personal data:name,
   timestamp=1523426910414, value=milind
row2 column=professional data:designation,
   timestamp=1523427061723, value=soft Engineer
row2 column=professional data:salary,
   timestamp=1523426965356, value=30000
row3 column=personal data:city,
   timestamp=1523428391129, value=4dehradun
row3 column=personal data:name,
   timestamp=1523427115249, value=anita
```

```
row3 column=professional data:designation,
   timestamp=1523427162000, value=tester
row3 column=professional data:salary,
   timestamp=1523427187838, value=40000
row3 column=xyz:city, timestamp=1523431975773,
   value=11nagpur
3 row(s) in 0.0620 seconds
```

Here, for scan command, the last updated value of 'xyz' column family is displayed i.e. city='nagpur'

9.2.5 Delete Command

TO DELETE A PARTICULAR COLUMN FAMILY

Whenever any changes are made to the table structure, we need to use Alter command. To execute Alter command, first table has to be disabled.

```
hbase(main):037:0> disable 'emp'
hbase(main):038:0> alter 'emp','delete'=>'xyz'
hbase(main):039:0> enable 'emp'
```

To verify whether column family has been deleted or not

```
hbase(main):042:0> get 'emp','row3'
```

```
OUTPUT:
COLUMN                                          CELL
personal data:city
   timestamp=1523428391129, value=4dehradun
personal data:name
   timestamp=1523427115249, value=anita
professional data:designation
   timestamp=1523427162000, value=tester
professional data:salary
   timestamp=1523427187838, value=40000
4 row(s) in 0.0080 seconds
```

TO DELETE A SPECIFIC CELL IN THE TABLE

Using the delete command, we can delete a specific cell in a table

Q) Remove the name 'Anita' from the table who is working as a tester.

```
hbase(main):045:0> delete 'emp','row3','personal
    data:name'
```

To Verify whether the cell has been deleted or not

```
hbase(main):046:0> get 'emp','row3'
```

```
OUTPUT:
COLUMN                                      CELL
personal data:city
    timestamp=1523428391129, value=4dehradun
professional data:designation
    timestamp=1523427162000, value=tester
professional data:salary
    timestamp=1523427187838, value=40000
3 row(s) in 0.1870 seconds
```

TO DELETE COMPLETE ROW IN TABLE

Using the "deleteall" command, we can delete all the cells in a row.

Q) Remove the entire details of the employee who is working as tester and his/her salary is Rs. 40000.

```
hbase(main):049:0> deleteall 'emp','row3'
```

To Verify whether the entire row has been deleted or not

```
hbase(main):050:0> get 'emp','row3'
```

```
OUTPUT:
COLUMN                                      CELL
0 row(s) in 0.0340 seconds
```

```
hbase(main):051:0> scan 'emp'
```

```
OUTPUT:
ROW                         COLUMN+CELL
row1 column=personal data:city,
    timestamp=1523426980414, value=hyd
```

```
row1 column=personal data:name,
    timestamp=1523426797711, value=raju
row1 column=professional data:designation,
    timestamp=1523426835511, value=manager
row1 column=professional data:salary,
    timestamp=1523426852045, value=50000
row2 column=personal data:city,
    timestamp=1523427018284, value=chennai
row2 column=personal data:name,
    timestamp=1523426910414, value=milind
row2 column=professional data:designation,
    timestamp=1523427061723, value=soft Engineer
row2 column=professional data:salary,
    timestamp=1523426965356, value=30000
2 row(s) in 0.0390 seconds
```

To count no:of rows availabale

```
hbase(main):052:0> count 'emp'
```

```
2 row(s) in 0.7080 seconds
```

9.2.6 Drop Command

It is used to delete the entire table along with its data and structure. Before dropping the table, it has to be disabled.

To list the available tables

```
hbase(main):005:0> list
```

```
TABLE
emp
example
exp
expert
```

To disable and drop the table 'emp'

```
hbase(main):024:0> disable 'emp'
hbase(main):001:0> drop 'emp'
```

To verify the drop

```
hbase(main):002:0> list
```

```
TABLE
example
exp
expert
```

To drop all three table which starts with name 'ex'

```
hbase(main):006:0> disable_all 'ex.*'
```

```
example
exp
expert

Disable the above 3 tables (y/n)?
y
3 tables successfully disabled
```

```
hbase(main):007:0> drop_all 'ex.*'
```

```
example
exp
expert

Drop the above 3 tables (y/n)?
y
3 tables successfully dropped
```